FIRE IN THE HILLS

Lee Fisher

*

INTRODUCTION BY
Billy Graham

ABINGDON PRESS
NASHVILLE   NEW YORK

FIRE IN

THE HILLS

*The Story of Parson Frakes
and the Henderson Settlement*

Fire in the Hills

Copyright © 1971 by Abingdon Press

ISBN 0-687-13080-8

Library of Congress Catalog Card Number: 73-134247

SET UP, PRINTED, AND BOUND BY THE
PARTHENON PRESS, AT NASHVILLE,
TENNESSEE, UNITED STATES OF AMERICA

To
Betty
my wife, who bravely
endured many a fracas
at Frakes, and who helped me
to organize the material
and type the manuscript for this
book

INTRODUCTION

*

Here is a story of real life on a missionary
frontier, as exciting and stimulating as any that could
come from the pen of a Hollywood fiction writer. It is ad-
ditional proof that "truth is stranger than fiction." The
mountain people of Appalachia are more than a legend—
they are a chunk of real Americana—and the Frakes story
shows what they can be when given a chance. Frakes
gave them that chance. "Called" from the comforts and
plaudits of a town parson to the rigors of transforming a
bloody valley in the Cumberland Mountains, he never once
complained of his lot. He gave, he sacrificed, and he
triumphed. And he did it, not single-handedly, but by the
"sword of the Spirit." But his was not a nebulous, un-
realistic ministry. He firmly believed that to save men's
souls was not the sum total of a parson. His "cup-of-cold-
water" doctrine found expression in better housing, better
education, better food, better roads, and better law en-
forcement. Surprisingly, to some, the transformation of
Laurel Fork demonstrated that exponents of the "old-
time religion" possess a social conscience. He weathered
the many storms of that tumultuous area because those
people knew he loved them. Today, in his eighties, he
is active and articulate—an effective oracle of God. Just
as adverse living conditions didn't deter him then, age is
no handicap now. This story is a sound argument that the
Gospel of Jesus Christ is not irrelevant. It never is when
it is given a chance. Frakes dared to expose a needy people
to its power—and it worked. It always does.

—Billy Graham

CONTENTS

*

*

1.

THE PARSON

Nestled in the picturesque Cumberland hill country, near Pineville, Kentucky, is a quiet, peaceful community called Frakes. This little community, spawned by faith and wrought by prayers, is the fulfillment of a dream, the pot of gold at the end of one man's rainbow. And that man is Hiram Frakes, a humble Methodist parson.

But Frakes, Kentucky, was not always Frakes, and Frakes himself was not always the man God meant him to be.

In studying the lives of great Christians, one cannot overlook the fact that God seems more interested in men who become tools in his hands than in men who would use him as a tool. Why didn't the Lord call Aaron, Moses' brother, to set His people free? Aaron was eloquent and articulate. He seemed all that a great emancipator should be. But no! Aaron was passed up for the stammering Moses, an unlikely prospect to be one of history's great men. Perhaps the Lord's strategy in using the ordinary to do the extraordinary is that he wants the world to know that it is "not by might, nor by power, but by my Spirit, saith the Lord."

So it was at the dawn of Christianity when the Lord Jesus Christ chose his disciples. What an unseemly lot they were. Not one of them was educated. None had the natural gifts for leadership. But when Christ touched them, commissioned them, and filled them with his Spirit, they turned the world upside down—and it has not been the same since.

When Peter and John healed a lame man on the temple

steps, the Scripture says of the crowd of five thousand who gathered there: "They . . . perceived that they were unlearned and ignorant men; . . . and they took knowledge of them that they had been with Jesus."

The hills around what is now known as Frakes once boomed with the sound of shotguns. Old-fashioned mountain feuding, complete with murders, was common. The ancestors of these hill people had carved out a little valley rich in soil and in coal. However, they lived by the rule of tooth and fang, because there was no road and no law. They made liquor for two reasons: they loved to drink it, and selling it gave them their bread and butter. But since good land was scarce, when the demand for a plot of ground to grow corn to make corn liquor became greater than the supply, then family turned on family, sometimes their own kinfolk, and the guns started blazing.

The Bell County law officers had long since written off "South America," as they called the area, as a social loss. "Aw, they're nothing but a bunch of robbers and murderers, and nothing will ever change them," was the consensus of opinion in Middlesboro.

No one was surprised when the sheriff would go into South America and bring back both the killer and the killed, dropping one off at the undertaker's, and the other off at the county jail. Trials usually were without witnesses, for fear of reprisals, and the sentences were brief for the same reason. South America, to the townspeople of Pineville and Middlesboro, was as far away—and as irrelevant—as that continent for which it was named.

Just as God prepared a Lincoln for the task of freeing the slaves; just as he prepared a General Booth to show compassion to the downtrodden of London's East End; and just as he prepared a Luther to spark the fires of the Reformation, he prepared a man to work among these forgotten people of the Cumberlands.

Like a homing pigeon with built-in radar, Hiram Frakes was unconsciously searching for his real niche in life. After his schooling, he graduated from the Dodge Institute of Telegraphy and became a telegraph operator for the Southern Railroad at English, Indiana. He worked in English for a time but was restless, so he transferred to the wheat fields of Kansas. Here he worked for awhile with an old friend from Indiana. After a short period here, he accepted a job as telegraph operator for the Santa Fe Railroad in Dodge City, Kansas. He then married his high school sweetheart, Leota Walker, from Indiana.

One evening Hiram and Leota were walking down the street in the little town of Holly, Colorado, where they had homesteaded some land. They had been given tickets for a picture show; but on the way to the theater they passed a large tent and heard singing inside. A sign announced that a "union revival" was in progress. They stood and listened to the spirited singing for a moment and then decided to attend the revival instead of the theater. The preacher gave the message "straight," and, when the altar call was given, they walked forward together without a word of consultation. The call of God reached each of them simultaneously, and they knelt together in the sawdust and accepted God's forgiveness into their lives. This night was the beginning of a complete revolution in the lives of Hiram Frakes and his wife Leota.

Interestingly enough, great movements often begin with small events that a news reporter wouldn't bother to write about. When John Wesley knelt at that little chapel in Aldersgate Street, the *London Times* carried no report of the event. But, later, the English historian Lecky said: "When John Wesley's heart was strangely warmed in Aldersgate, it was a national epoch."

Few, perhaps, took notice of that young couple kneeling in contrition before the Lord that night in that small town in Colorado; but the good Lord in heaven was very aware. He had spoken to Frakes's heart first; but, more than that, he had plans for Frakes, and this night was an important part of that plan. It was the beginning!

While Hiram Frakes had been brought up in a Method-ist church and had never been a hell-raisin' sinner, he had finally reached a point in his life that all spiritual leaders reach. He realized he was too weak to face life without a personal relationship with God. Frakes went out of that revival service that night with a lighter step, a glow on his face, and a joy he had never known before in his heart. He was a new man! Some time was yet to elapse before he found his "people" to liberate; but that night, in the sawdust, he enrolled in the Lord's training school, and life for him would never be the same again. The old song, "I'll go where you want me to go, . . . I'll be what you want me to be," kept ringing in his ears. It was so much on his mind that he found himself whistling it as he went about his work. It seemed to express his desire those days, and it showed in his work.

The telegraph work continued, but a new dimension had been added. He just had to share his newfound joy which God had given him with others. He studied his Bible and began to preach whenever he was invited, and in time he was granted a local preacher's license by the Southeast Kansas Conference. The Lord had to move him around like a checker in the hands of a master player, but He finally got him in position for the "key" move.

At first Frakes felt a strong pull back to southern Indiana. He took a job for the Monon Railroad at Quincy and became very involved in the church there. He was made Sunday school superintendent; and it was in Quincy that he completed the four-year course of study for the ministry. The Indiana Conference then granted him deacon's orders. His first actual church appointment was in the Methodist church in Lanesville, Indiana. All of these events were related, although at the time they may have seemed unrelated. He had to go to Colorado to get converted. He had to go to Kansas to get his preacher's license. He had to go to Indiana to get his study course and his first assignment as a minister; but he hadn't discovered God's ultimate plan yet. He was coming nearer to the center of God's will, though, when he noticed one day that one of the District Superintendents in Kentucky was asking for preachers with a missionary spirit to come to the mountains to minister to the coal camps. This was Hiram's cup of tea, and he immediately applied for a job. That summer he was assigned to Benham, Kentucky, where he was to be the pastor at a coal camp.

A year later, when his superintendent, Ollie G. Ragan, saw the leadership qualities of Frakes, along with his dedication, he sent him to the First Methodist Church of Pineville as pastor. Frakes served this congregation well for three years; but down deep he knew he had not reached his "Bethel." Daily he searched his soul and sought to learn from God his will in life. God heard his prayers and gradually directed him to his final life's work.

So it was that in 1925 the Rev. Hiram Frakes entered a packed courtroom in Pineville, Kentucky, to attend a murder trial. Throughout the three years in hill country, Hiram had been no stranger to courtroom proceedings. As secretary for the local church's social service work he had come to grips with every kind of human problem —from petty theft to murder. Like his Master he had a compassion for the poor, the brokenhearted, and those held captives by sin. He was drawn like a magnet to scenes of human suffering. It must have been so, for he didn't know the exact reason he tiptoed into that courtroom on that cold February day. He only knew that the judge, one of his church members, was presiding over a murder hearing in the county courtroom and he felt a strong urge to be there.

Seated in the front rows of the courtroom were clusters of gloomy-faced mountaineers—tall and gaunt and sullen. In ominous silence they stared defiantly back at the bench, their horny hands tucked into overall suspenders and their bearded jowls chewing in rhythmic unison on tobacco cuds. For two days now they had sat thus, motionless as statues, mum as mutes. A particularly vicious feud had flared up in their section, about twenty miles away. They had been summoned as witnesses. With the help of their testimony the court had hoped to fix blame for some of the killings that had taken place. A hope, it developed, as optimistic as it was vain. Small wonder then that the judge's patience had burst its seams.

As the Methodist minister entered the courtroom, he noted that his friend the presiding judge was unusually disturbed and his face was flushed from anger.

"All right!" he shouted, "you won't talk. You won't brand the criminals. You won't help establish law and order in your community so your children can have a decent chance at life. I suggest you all go back home to your South America and shoot and maim and murder until you're all killed off. Then we will come in and establish a civil government. Court's adjourned!"

The judge banged his gavel with a vengeance, disgust written all over his face. He was tired of trying to help these people who seemed to have no desire to help themselves.

The silent men of the mountains shuffled to their feet slowly and, almost insolently, walked from the courtroom. As the last one passed through the door, the judge turned to see Hiram Frakes beside him.

"Howdy, parson," he said. "Sorry you caught me backsliding with such an unsanctified temper, but those—"

The preacher interrupted.

"I've been hearing a lot about that South America clan lately, Judge. Everybody says it's the worst spot in the United States for moonshining and feuding."

"In the world, you mean," the judge amended. "There's not an adult male in the whole ten square miles out there who isn't engaged in making illicit liquor, and more people have been killed in feuds out there than in all the rest of Kentucky put together."

The judge wiped the sweat from his forehead and continued. "Two-thirds of all the cases before this court come from South America, and we get a conviction only once in a blue moon."

A few days after his conversation with the judge, without confiding his mission to anyone, Frakes started for South America. A coal train took him as far as Chenoa, a mining camp at the end of the line. It was six miles farther to his destination. As he entered the valley, he met two surly mountaineers, who looked him over, decided he was a revenue agent or a reasonable facsimile, and moved off to spread the word.

He knocked at several doors before he found one open to him. The woman who opened the door was shy and suspicious. Not many outsiders found their way into the valley, and when they did, they were usually law officers, and they weren't welcome.

The woman told him to walk down the trail and he would probably meet someone to help him. Three miles down the mountain path he met a man who was a lookout for a moonshine operation. Frakes told him his mission: that he wanted to establish a Christian school for the children of that community. The mountaineer considered this for a few moments, and then said in his slow drawl, "Well, now I reckin I'd better go along. If you are who you say you are, maybe I can help ye. If you're not, me and my pony can come back alone."

That was the wedge, the start, the beginning. But there were many more trails to follow, many more mountains to climb, and many more rivers to cross.

2.

THE START OF A DREAM

The Parson and the mountaineer started up the twisting mountain trail. Thin wisps of fog clustered above the little coves, and smoke ascended from the tiny cabins perched on the sides of steep slopes. As their horses jaunted along, the Parson said, "We've got to find a suitable spot for our school and church."

"It won't be easy," said the mountaineer. "There ain't much level land in these parts, and the folks that has it don't take much to sellin' it."

"I don't want to buy it," Frakes said. "I want these people to give me the land for a school—and they're going to do it."

The mountaineer looked up at the Parson with a silly grin and shyly retorted, "You're jest crazy enough to believe thet, hain't you!"

As they walked beside their horses up a steep grade, the Parson unveiled his plans to the stranger. "I want a lot of land—a hundred acres or more. I want pasture to graze cattle on, so we'll have our own milk and butter for the children who live too far away to walk to school every day. I want some flat land for a dormitory, a school, a church, a barn, and some chicken houses."

His guide, whom he later found out was a moonshiner's lookout, was taken in by the little man with the shining eyes and the bold dream. "I know a place," he volunteered, "if'n you can git ahold of it." Pointing up a steep trail, he said, "it's jest over thet hill yonder."

As they came to the summit, Frakes couldn't believe his eyes. Below him stretched one of the greenest and fairest valleys he had ever seen. It was like some fabled Brigadoon in the Scottish Highlands. There were groves and fields and meadows. He shut his eyes briefly. He could envision a white school building with happy children running in and out and a steepled church with worshipers entering a spotless sanctuary, and the end of violence and feuding which had beleagured these bloody hills for years. A prayer crossed his lips: "O God, I don't know how you're going to do it, but give this valley to me, and I'll nourish it like a Garden of Eden."

Frakes then looked at his guide like a man awakening from a vision. And shaking himself to reality, he said, "I told you I have no money; but—" He remembered his prayer, "But will you take me to the people who own this land anyway?"

Slowly leading the way, the man first took him to Uncle Scott Partin. He was the senior "shiner," who boasted that his grandfather had accompanied Daniel Boone into Kentucky. Uncle Scott had just returned to the Laurel Creek section after a seven-year visit to the state penitentiary for his participation in a violent feud. When the Parson told him enthusiastically about his almost impossible dream for Laurel Creek, the old man looked him over from head to toe appraisingly. He glanced again at his small parcel of lush land and, like a man with a shotgun pressed against his ribs, said with a sigh, "Okay, you can count on me for sixteen acres—if yer gonna' do what you say you are."

The second man they approached about adding to their gift of land said, "Preacher, I ain't got no money, I ain't got no larnin', and I ain't got no land to speak of, only five acres to my name." Then he paused and hesitatingly added, "But half of it is yourn, if you'll help our kids to get some larnin'."

With this beginning, word of the proposed project got around fast. Though there were no phones or tom-tom drums, news traveled fast in mountain areas. Frakes hadn't been in the Laurel Creek community but a few hours, but almost everyone there was aware of his presence.

The next man he contacted was Bill Henderson. Bill was known throughout those mountains as the "King of the Moonshiners." Legally, the county was "dry." But just as the mountain dew forms upon the shrubs and fields of Laurel Creek in the night, another kind of "mountain dew," made from corn squeezings, was conjured up during the hours of darkness. Moonshine was simply a "nice thing for passing the time" for the drinkers of Pineville and Middlesboro, but it was a necessity for these hill people. At least they thought so. They looked upon the manufacture of the stuff as an economic opportunity. And Bill Henderson operated the biggest still in the valley.

When he met Henderson, Frakes knew he must handle the man carefully. His guide had told him that Bill counted his misdemeanors against the law by notches on his gun—and those notches numbered thirteen! Just so, there were thirteen indictments lodged against him at the courthouse in Pineville. He was the titular head of a feuding clan, revered by his clansmen, feared by his enemies, and sought constantly by the police. His trusty shooting iron stood between him and apprehension by the law. But Bill Henderson had a soft spot in his heart, his children. He loved them dearly and coveted for them a better chance in life than he had had. Bill owned sixty-eight acres of land, and it comprised a large part of the portion that had first caught Frakes's eye. It was the most valuable land in the entire area.

Frakes decided to approach Bill Henderson just as he had the others, in honesty and openness. He told him of his dream for the valley and challenged him for the sake of his wife and children to be a part of it. Bill listened intently as Frakes described Laurel Creek as it could be, and when Frakes finished, Bill eyed him silently for a long interval. Then he stood up, shoved his hands in the pockets of his overalls, threw back his shoulders, and said, "Preacher, I don't do things halfway. When I'm sold on something, I'm sold all the way. I'll just give you the whole sixty-eight acres!"

Frakes couldn't believe his ears. Shocked, because he'd heard even in Pineville about the meanness of Bill Henderson, he asked for affirmation. "Do you mean you're going to give all the land you own?"

"Yep, that's what I mean," Bill assured him. He went on, "I know my days are numbered, preacher. The law is after me hard; and if, when they git me, you'll take care of my kids, the land is yours."

For three months Frakes had been convinced over and over again that he had done right by resigning his church in Pineville and coming to Laurel Fork. Now that conviction was established for a lifetime. He had never been so excited about anything in all his years.

During these three months he had seen miracle after miracle unfold before his very eyes. He had lived with the people and visited nearly all of them in their humble cabins, talking to their children, learning their names, and gradually winning their confidence. They had come to accept him and believe in him, and that was the greatest miracle of all.

Yes, he knew there was lots of moonshining going on. In fact, he had learned that it could well be the leading source of income in the valley. But he did not take the role of "informer," preferring rather to handle the issue by seeing the people changed on the inside by Christian conversion. It would take time; but he figured that both he and God had lots of that—and he believed with all his heart that eventually the change would come.

Having received the "go" signal from the people of Laurel Fork, Frakes was now ready to challenge the leaders of his church to match the sacrifices of the poor people of the valley. So in the spring he went to Cincinnati to lay his proposition before his resident bishop, Bishop Theodore S. Henderson.

The Bishop welcomed him heartily. He had looked forward to this meeting, for he was anxious to hear all about this new project that Frakes had written about so enthusiastically. Soon the Bishop's desk could not accommodate all the maps, drawings, and photographs that Frakes had brought; so they spread the materials out on the floor. Together they got down on the floor so they could better go over all the plans that Frakes had in mind. The Bishop was impressed by the careful, methodical survey the parson had made.

Frakes findings revealed: There were 1,248 children within a radius of six miles; the few who did go to school were dropping out at the third and fourth grades; the girls were marrying at twelve and thirteen years of age; the boys were invariably following their fathers into moonshining; and life expectancy was amazingly low because of feuds. All these evils existed because of the lack of proper training in religion, education, health, and economic and social opportunity.

Frakes convinced the Bishop that he was ready, able, and willing to dedicate his life to improving conditions in those hills. With his natural-born streak of Hoosier independence, he didn't even ask the Bishop for funds or conference support. "All I want," he told the Bishop, "is the opportunity to sell this project to the churches of our denomination." He went on to say that he was ready to stake his whole future on his ability to do so, by the grace of God.

As the two men stood amidst the jumble of maps, charts, and pictures on the floor, the Bishop put his hand on Frakes's shoulder and said, "Brother Frakes, you certainly have my blessing. I'm with you all the way. I want you to return to your mission field, secure a place for you and Mrs. Frakes to live, and then—eat, sleep, and live with this dream."

Frakes now had three things essential to the materialization of his God-given vision: (1) The inner consciousness that he was in the will of God; (2) The cooperation of the people of Laurel Fork as evidenced by their sacrificial giving of their land; and (3) The blessing of the titular head of his denomination.

It appeared that there was smooth sledding ahead. But even Frakes himself, who now probably knew these hill people better than anyone else, little realized the obstacles ahead. Some would be so great as to threaten to destroy his hopes and dreams for these forgotten people.

3.

IF ANY LACK WISDOM

Lack of education, not ignorance, was the bugaboo of the hills. Frakes believed strongly in the scripture, "Seek ye first the kingdom of God and his righteousness, and all these things shall be added unto you." But he also believed that knowledge was important to the full development of the human personality, and a school was a big part of his original dream for the valley.

The county authorities had neglected this remote section because of fear. They knew that every outsider was considered a criminal intruder, and that few schoolteachers were dedicated enough to be the slightest bit interested in teaching at the Settlement. In fact, the chairman of the county school board had said, when Frakes approached him about a school in Laurel Fork: "Can't do it. It's too dangerous to try that sort of thing in that section."

The Bible says, "But God hath chosen the foolish things of the world to confound the wise; and God hath chosen the weak things of the world to confound the things which are mighty" (I Cor. 1:27). Frakes himself was limited in education, having never attended a seminary. So for this and obvious other reasons he wanted his valley parishioners to have the benefit of wisdom and knowledge. He well knew that lack of education was the cause of many of the feuds and much of the killing. He was convinced that if the people could get God in their hearts and Christian wisdom in their heads the valley could be transformed.

But few of his confidants seemed to share his conviction. Everyone he talked to agreed that the need was indeed present, but their apathy was only exceeded by their hopelessness and despair of the situation. Frakes, always remembering his dream for these people, proceeded with the faith that somehow, sometime, God would provide a way. He knew that God was the sponsor of his project, and that God didn't sponsor failures.

One day, as his wagon rounded a bend in the trail from the coal camp, Frakes met a nicely dressed woman in a wagon. To his surprise she jumped out and said, "You must be the preacher I've heard so much about. I'm here to help you!"

Frakes was dumbfounded. Either this woman was demented or she was totally unaware of conditions in Laurel Fork. To the men who lived in these hills a woman was a chattel, a necessary piece of household equipment and nothing more. They did not think of a woman as being qualified for any kind of leadership.

Unaware of any such obstacles, the smiling lady from the "outside" said, "I came to help you with your school. I'm a graduate of the Chicago Training School and a deaconess in The Methodist Church. I heard about your project away up in Chicago, and, after I'd prayed about it for several weeks, I knew God wanted me to come and help you. So here I am."

Frakes still was not quite able to grasp what was happening. Fumbling for words, he said, "That's wonderful, but it's impossible. I have no place for you to live, no funds for the school, no money to pay you with, and I'm not sure the people would take kindly to a woman."

Frakes thought this would conclude the matter; but not so. Here was a woman to whom God had given a piece of his vision, and who was an answer to his prayer, although he did not know it yet, and she could not be dissuaded.

"What's that old building over there?" she asked.

Frakes's eyes followed her pointing finger. "Oh, that's nothing but an old log stable. There's a cow and a calf in there, and it's unfit for human habitation."

"Why, Mr. Frakes," Bertha Riel—for that was her name —retorted, "wasn't the One we serve born in a stable? And couldn't he fill that cow stable with his presence just as he hallowed that lowly stable in Bethlehem two thousand years ago?"

Frakes was duly and effectively rebuked. Here was a woman with the insight and courage that he needed for the work in Laurel Fork. He was not about to fight her help, if she was serious.

Miss Riel, seeing her point had gotten to him, went on, "With the aid of gallons of water and pounds of soap we'll get this stable cleaned out, and I'll be able to live in it. And we can start our school."

Frakes's heart was jumping with excitement; but he felt impelled to warn this unseasoned woman of the dangers involved. He told her of the violence and lawlessness, of the hate and ignorance. When he had had his say, he looked at her and saw that nothing he said had any effect on her spirits. Instead, she interrupted him, saying, "Now, Mr. Frakes, I've heard about all that already. I didn't come here entirely ignorant of the situation; but that's why this work is so challenging. All I want to do now is to get on with it."

"But what about your salary?" Frakes queried.

"What's your salary?" Miss Riel asked in response.

"I don't get any."

"Then put me down for the same income until we begin to get on our feet. I'll eat what you eat, I'll sleep in this stable, and we'll work together for the fulfillment of God's plan for these people."

That is the way the first school started. Frakes said that he turned the cow and calf out, and turned Miss Riel in. She started a Sunday school in that cabin the next Sunday, and she used the little cabin—which she'd scrubbed as clean and neat as a proper mountain house— for social gatherings for the young people, in addition to living in it.

Now with a school building and a schoolteacher, and

one duly qualified too, Frakes set out to round up his school pupils. The only school they had had before he came (it had been closed down for some time) was too small, a roughly built plank house twelve by fourteen feet. There were no seats or desks. The only furniture and supplies were crude benches made from unplaned lumber and three schoolbooks for the eleven children who attended. Frakes found that there were eighty-eight children in the immediate vicinity of the Settlement who should have been in school. A large percentage of the eighty-eight were married, many of them only twelve-, thirteen-, or fourteen-year-olds. They married because their parents had large families and had to make room for the new babies which came along every year or oftener. Three families in Laurel Fork provided forty-five children for the Settlement school eventually.

Most of the adults could not read or write, and the educational level of the school-age children would have been about second or third grade. One little girl who came to school the first day, when asked what grade she was in, said, "I've been halfway through the fourth grade four times."

When asked what she meant, she said, "Our teacher could not go any farther than halfway through the fourth grade himself, and he would turn us back when we got that far. So I went halfway through the fourth grade four times."

One day the children came running in to Miss Riel and said, "Mr. Banks is here. Come out and see him. He's right out there in the yard."

"Who is Mr. Banks?" Miss Riel asked the children.

"He's our mountain schoolteacher."

Mr. Banks had heard there was a modern school in Laurel Fork and, though past eighty years of age, had walked several miles across the ridge to see the new school. Miss Riel invited him in to speak to the children.

He said he would rather not. "You see," he said, "I ain't got no larnin' like you got, and I ain't comin' in."

27

"But aren't you a schoolteacher?" asked Miss Riel.

"Yes'm," he answered. "I've been larnin' our boys and girls nigh onto forty years in these here mountains."

After a little persuasion he consented to go inside and talk to the pupils. He told them, "Now, boys and girls, get all the larnin' you can. This h'yar good woman has come down from the North to larn you'uns a lot of things I couldn't larn you."

Then he turned to the blackboard and looked at the problem that had been worked there before recess. He looked at it for a few moments and said, "I see you been doin' a problem h'yar. Now that's beyond me. I couldn't work that. I'm mighty proud of ya'."

The problem was a standard fourth-grade problem.

One day in February, one of the handymen at the Settlement went into Pineville to transact some business. He could neither read nor write, for he had never spent a day in school. When he returned, he looked a little downcast, and another worker asked him if he'd gotten his business taken care of.

"Nope," he said. Some big shot in Pineville was celebrating his birthday, and I guess everybody went to the party, 'cause everything were closed."

"What was his name?" the fellow worker asked.

"Hit was some guy named Washington. I never did larn his first name. Everyone I ast about the stores all bein' closed jest said, 'It's Washington's birthday.'"

When Frakes first went out to work at the Settlement, he still kept his house in Pineville for quite awhile until he could get one built in Laurel Fork suitable for his wife. On one of his trips home he decided to take Alice, one of the mountain girls, with him, for she had never been out of the valley.

When they arrived at his home, he and his wife found real pleasure in showing Alice the modern conveniences of city life. She was wide-eyed as Frakes showed her how to push the little black button to turn the lights on. Then he showed her how to turn on the faucet in the sink. She stood on a chair, giggling, turning the faucet on and off and letting the warm water run over her hands.

They took her upstairs and showed her the modern bathroom. When her eyes fell on the tub, in wonderment she looked up at the Parson and exclaimed, "Mr. Frakes, what are you doin' with that white horse trough in h'yar?"

For her, seeing Frakes's house was like going to the fair and having free admission to all the shows. She wanted to see it all. They took her to the basement, and she went into the furnace room, looked at the furnace, and saw the fire inside. She stood back in fear; but they assured her that she need not be afraid and explained it was just a stove that furnished the heat for the house. Her eyes literally began to dance as she gleefully said, "Oh, Mr. Frakes, wouldn't this be a dandy place for a moonshine still?"

Alice was not ignorant, she was illiterate. She was representative of the 1,200 children in "South America" (the Laurel Fork section), who had been insulated and isolated from the outside world. For one hundred years there had never been in that valley a farm agent, a home agent, a social worker, a sanitary officer, a government official, or a county welfare worker. Talk about the plight of the blacks! These white people lived in squalor equal to or worse than any blacks in the poorest ghettos of our cities. And no one had championed their cause—except Parson Frakes. They loved him for it. It wasn't welfare they wanted. They wanted a chance to fend for themselves, and Frakes was determined to give them that chance.

The school term started off in 1925 with thirteen students. Every day saw improvement in the students' physical appearance and their mental attitudes. Miss Riel, they soon found, was one of the best friends they could have. She had come to do the noblest of all tasks: to put love in their hearts by the grace of God, and to put knowledge in their heads.

Of those first thirteen students, Wayland Jones went on to graduate from high school and from Union College.

He lives in Frakes at the present time and teaches in the high school.

Ethel Bowlin-Brown graduated from the Settlement High School, attended college, and came back to teach for several years at the Settlement. She later married a schoolteacher and moved to Jellico, Tennessee, where she is teaching in the school system and her husband is a successful businessman.

Mossie Murray-Price graduated from high school, entered college, and married; Florence Bowlin graduated from high school and married a schoolteacher; Minerva Partin graduated from high school, attended Berea College, and became a graduate nurse with an R. N. certificate from Cook County Hospital, Chicago. She is still there nursing.

The others obtained an elementary education at least; they married, obtained gainful employment, or went into business for themselves. Not one fell into the old mountain pattern of "marry, feud, make moonshine, and die." Even from the first, Frakes's dream took shape, and his vision found fulfillment.

4.

THE FIRST CHRISTMAS

Pineville and Middlesboro, due to their isolation, had their share of lawlessness. A murder a week was about par for those two towns in Bell County. But conditions at Laurel Fork were far worse. Situated sixteen miles from Pineville, thirty-five miles from Middlesboro, with nothing but an ungraded, deep-rutted, rocky trail for a road, Laurel Fork was too far away for the law to matter, it seemed. Here young men and old died violently —usually at gunpoint—over the most trifling differences. Making their own laws, families exacted endless reprisals stemming from the only code they knew: "An eye for an eye, and a tooth for a tooth." Each man feared his neighbor, never knowing when a shot might ring out, accompanied by the burning pain of a penetrating bullet, signalling the end of his life on earth.

This more than anything else was what Frakes prayed to help change. He knew it had to have first priority, if for no other reason, for the children. He once observed to a friend in Pineville, "Those kids are living like wildcats."

One thing he knew, he could not do the job alone. He needed help and plenty of it. He had the land and the approval of his denomination. Now he needed people to implement his dream for his adopted hill country.

Winter was coming on, many of the men were out of work, and clothing and food were scarce. The large families living in the substandard cabins would be hard put to withstand the cold of another winter.

As Frakes thought of this problem, an idea was sparked,

and he started to work on it. There were doubtless hundreds of churches throughout Methodism who would gladly contribute food and secondhand clothing if they were asked.

That night, by lamplight, he wrote the resident bishop in Cincinnati about the problem. He had come to know that Bishop Henderson had a soft spot in his heart for the Settlement and its people. He felt sure the Bishop would help.

The good Bishop reacted with a personal letter to many of the large churches within the area of his jurisdiction. In a matter of weeks barrels of clothing began to roll in, and boxes of food. So generous was the response that space for storage became an immediate problem. The old clapboard building down by the log post office was turned into a "general store." The clothing was sorted, racks were made by the Settlement carpenter, and food was displayed in the "grocery."

Frakes knew these people to be an independent lot who would not take kindly to charity; so in order to keep everyone happy he put a price on everything just like a city store—except the prices were scaled down to conform to the Settlement economy. Shoes were 50¢ a pair; overcoats were $1.50; and dresses went up to 88¢. Food was dispensed similarly. A can of beans was 3¢, a pound of coffee 10¢, and a sack of flour 8¢.

Business boomed from the beginning. The mountain people found it a treat to be able to "shop." They left the store with their bundles of clothing and sacks of food and felt as if they had been to town. Frakes knew he had found a good combination: the need of his people matched by the generosity of concerned Christians far and near.

The mountain people were not style-conscious, for they were not in position to know what the latest styles were. Some of their "git-ups" were quite extraordinary, as their purchases of clothing ran to the ribald and ridiculous. A red satin "flapper" skirt, discarded by some conscience-stricken Methodist woman, worn with a pair of 1902 high-button shoes and a tailored, plaid flannel blouse was not unusual. As far as these people were concerned, these clothes sent to them by the city folk were the latest and most chic styles—and they were as pleased as punch.

When the Christmas season arrived, it was announced that the school would have a Christmas tree and a Christmas program and all the people in the valley were invited. When one mountaineer heard of it, he said, "Now I heerd of a oak tree, a elm tree, a maple tree, and a gum tree; but I swanee if I ever heerd of a Christmas tree!"

It was a cold, rainy day when the time for the special event arrived, but many family groups could be seen trudging down the wet, muddy road and the narrow lanes that led to the former cow stable. There was very little to look forward to in the once-forsaken valley, and these people were not going to miss seeing a Christmas tree, of all things!

Friends of the Settlement had sent colorfully wrapped gifts, and the churches of Pineville had sent generous sacks of candy for each one attending. Miss Riel put her own scant assortment of decorations on the tree and pinned the packages on the empty branches. She spread the candy around the bottom like a colorful skirt. Then so as to whet the curiosity a little more, she covered it all with a large white sheet.

There was an air of mystery and excitement as the time to view the tree approached. Gathered together for the festive occasion were aproned mothers with babies in their arms and little ones clinging to their skirts. There were boys and girls and teen-agers alike waiting eagerly for the magic moment. There were fathers and grandfathers steeling their faces to hide the excitement they felt.

No one at the program that day—and there were at least a hundred people—had ever seen a Christmas tree. Finally the highly anticipated moment arrived! Bertha Riel slipped over to the tree and slowly pulled off its covering, and there in its tinseled beauty stood the grand vision of green, white, and red. A ripple of admiring sighs came from the thrilled group. And, when they were able to find their voices, each exclaimed in his own way his own personal feeling about the tree. It was surely the prettiest thing they had ever seen. The Parson slowly lit the candles as they all watched in enthralled silence. Then the gifts and goodies were passed to the crowd. It was a very special time for these shy and usually restrained people. Laughter was rife, and a joy they had never known in fellowship had come to them.

The Christmas party with its program was the first public meeting ever held in the valley up until that time in which there was no incident of violence or rowdyism. He who brought "peace on earth and goodwill toward men" had come to this isolated community. Three years previously, some of the people had tried to have a public meeting; but there was so much moonshining and drinking and gun-toting that they had not dared try again. But on this Christmas Day there was not a pistol seen in the crowd. One lady exclaimed as she left the school with happiness in her heart and gifts in her hands, "What a wonderful new day has come to us at Laurel Fork."

5.

BIG, BAD BILL HENDERSON

The Parson's years at Laurel Fork were like the weather the good Lord gives, a mixture of clouds and sunshine, of rain and fair weather. A victory would be gained, only to be followed by some kind of discouraging incident. At the very time of the glorious Christmas party, Bill Henderson, the man with the big heart and the notorious reputation, was hiding in the mountains near his home, a fugitive from justice. There was a reward of $200 for his capture. Parson Frakes felt strongly that something had to be done about Bill. Bill had given sixty-eight acres to the project of Henderson Settlement, and most of the people in the valley, and in Pineville as well, thought it had been named for him alone. They of course didn't know about the good bishop with the same name. But getting Bill leveled off was no cinch.

Frakes, having conducted jail services in Pineville from time to time when Bill Henderson was an inmate, had become fascinated with this contradiction of a man. Since Henderson seemed to be perennially in jail, Frakes had good opportunities to study him. It was always Bill who would say to the other inmates, "Come on, boys, the Parson is here, and we must give him our respects."

One Sunday, after Frakes had talked with the prisoners, a young man stepped forward to accept Christ. Bill Henderson, to everyone's surprise, was the first to shake the young prisoner's hand and to congratulate him for his courageous step. This is to say that like all of us Bill had a good and a bad side. This gave Frakes both concern and, at the same time, hope for Bill.

Henderson was serving one of his jail sentences just before an election was to take place, and the jailer was up for re-election. The jailer told Bill that he would forget to lock the cell one night if Bill would agree to go back to Laurel Fork and electioneer for him. So one night the jailer did just that: he "forgot" to lock Bill's cell with the thought that Bill would slip out and go home and campaign for him. Bill did go home; but instead of campaigning for the jailer who freed him, he campaigned for his opponent, whom he apparently thought was a more honest man. I suppose Bill thought that any jailer who would forget to lock a cell was unworthy to be the turnkey for the county.

When the new jailer was installed, he tried in every way possible to get Bill to come back on his own and finish his sentence, but Bill dogmatically refused. One day the jailer saw Frakes in town and asked him if he ever saw Bill Henderson in Laurel Fork.

Frakes answered, "I see him every day or so, and just last week I spent the night at his place."

"If you'll bring him in," the jailer said, "I've got a $200 reward for you."

Frakes quickly told the officer that he was not a law officer but a minister of the Gospel, and if Bill were brought in, the jailer would have to do it himself.

Not long after that, four deputy sheriffs armed with high-powered rifles went out to Laurel Fork one night to get Bill so they could claim the reward for his capture. They went to Bill's barn and kept under cover until daylight. At dawn, Bill walked out of his cabin with his trusty shooting iron in his hands and a pistol dangling in a holster. As he came through the yard gate, one of the officers crawled from under the barn and, with his gun drawn, said, "Okay, Uncle Bill, wait right there. We want to have a talk with you."

Henderson, quickly sizing up the situation, said, "All right, boys, just wait. I'll be back in a minute." And with that he darted toward the door of his house to take cover, at least momentarily. When he made a break for the cabin, all four officers let go with a barrage of shots, peppering the house.

When all seemed quiet and there had been no sound from Bill in some time, one of the officers asked the other men to cover him; he walked cautiously up to the cabin door with his gun ready. Here he encountered Bill's wife, as she slowly opened the door to peer out and see what was happening.

"Where's Bill?" the officer asked.

"I dunno'," she answered. "I guess you killed him."

The officer, sensing that she might be giving him the runaround, said, "We want to come in and search for moonshine."

"If ye have a warrant, you can," she answered wisely. "I know you lawmen! You slip into a person's house, place some liquor under the bed, and then pull it out and say ye found it there. No, ye're not comin' in exceptin' over my dead body." Convinced now that they were not going to gain entry to the cabin or apprehend Henderson that day, the men returned to Pineville.

The next day Frakes, who had heard about the incident, saw Bill and asked, "Bill, how did you manage to keep from being hit by those sixteen rounds from the deputies' bullets?"

"Oh," Bill said, "I just jumped first this way and then t'other way, so they couldn't hit me till I got in the house. Then I slipped out the side door and finally fell down over a big stone and rolled under a little ledge where I could see everything that happened.

"Parson," Bill continued, "I could have killed any one of those men—I had 'em dead in my sight. But then I thought of all you been doin' fer me to git me out o' trouble, and I dropped my aim. I knew if I kilt one of them fellers, everything you've done fer me would be ruint."

In an all-out effort to persuade Bill to volunteer to go back to jail before the officers came back again, the Parson

made arrangements to meet Bill at his brother's house
after nightfall. He realized that all attempts to get a
pardon for Bill were futile as long as Bill was a fugitive
from justice. The two met at Bill's brother's cabin, hidden
in a ravine, and talked long into the night.

Along toward morning a violent storm began brewing.
The thunder and lightning rocked the little cabin as the
men talked. There was no way for Bill and Frakes to
leave, as the rain began to pour. "Well, I guess ye'll be
spending the night," Bill's brother announced.

"Yes, I guess we'll hav' ta," Bill said, "if'n ye got some-
place to put us up."

"All I've got is that old lean-to with one bed in it,"
his brother answered, "but you're welcome to that."

Frakes said, "I can stand it if Bill can, I guess."

Bill looked at Frakes warily and mumbled, "I've slept
with dogs, sheep, en' cows. I guess I kin sleep with a
parson."

Bill pulled a rickety chair close to the side of the old
bed, took his holster off, and hung it over the back. Then,
he stood "Ole Betsie," his faithful shooting iron, up
against the head of the bed. Thus amply protected for the
night, they blew the candle out and lay down with their
clothes still on their bodies.

In the darkness Bill said to the Parson, "I guess you
wonder about all this artillery, but, ye see, I never know
when they're a-comin' after me."

Frakes had been talking to Bill all evening about the
terrible, insecure way of his life, and he knew Bill was in
no mood for any more preaching, so he kept quiet; besides he was ready for some sleep.

A few days later, Frakes went again to see Bill at his
cabin with the opportunity for a parole for Bill still very
much on his mind. Bill's wife answered the door and said
that Bill was in the back field "a-grubbin'" some sprouts
out so he could plant corn. Frakes went to find Bill, and
when he spotted him, he saw that his fourteen-year-old
daughter Ruth was with him to watch out for anyone who

might try to kill him. Ruth was sitting on the old stone fence, looking first one direction then the other. Frakes realized again that Bill had lived for years in constant fear that someone would beat him to the draw.

Frakes decided to face the issue head on, so he went to where Bill was working and said, "Bill, aren't you tired of living as a fugitive? You know I'm your friend, and I have an idea that if you'll give yourself up now we can get you cleared. I'm trying to help you. Don't you think it's about time you gave me some cooperation?"

Bill must have been having the same thoughts, for he offered no resistance this time. "All right, Parson, I guess yer' right," he said. "How ya' goin' to build this here school you talk about, and that church, if'n I keep running from the law." He picked up his high-powered rifle and turned to his daughter and said, "Come on, kid, let's you and me go to the house. Your dad and the Parson has got some important business to do."

No words were spoken as the three walked single file on the little path that led to Bill's cabin. Each in his own way realized that a monumental decision had been made. As they reached the open door of the cabin, Bill called out to his wife, "Old woman, git me some clean overalls. I'm a-goin' to town."

Apprehensively she said, "What fer?"

"By gonnies, I'm goin' to jail. The Parson has made me believe he kin hep me better if'n I go to jail than if'n I stay out."

Because the Parson didn't want it to look like an arrest, Bill hiked the four miles to Chenoa Junction all alone, and took the 1:30 P.M. coal train to Pineville. He walked into the county jail, marched up to the turnkey, and said, "Okay, here I am. Lock me up."

The Parson was now in a bargaining position, and he went to work. A petition asking the governor to give Bill a full and free pardon was carried to Bill's neighbors. Not a neighbor refused to sign. Those who were a bit reluctant signed for fear Bill would hold it against them if and when he got out. Then a similar petition was signed by the county officials, because he had come in of his own free will, and because Frakes had convinced them that Bill would straighten up and become a good citizen.

Frakes then made a trip to Frankfort to present his petitions to the governor. Seated across the desk from the governor, Frakes began his plea for Bill. The first setback came immediately, for the governor showed the Parson a telegram from one of the county officials who had refused to sign the petition. He asked the governor to refuse the Parson's request.

"Yes, Governor," Frakes said, "I'm not surprised at that; but from my personal knowledge, some of our county officials are worse than Bill. They buy whiskey from him, which only encourages him to go on producing the illegal stuff."

The governor agreed that he was probably right about that. Then he looked the Parson straight in the eye and said, "Frakes, you and I both know that Bill Henderson is one of the most notorious outlaws in the mountains." You say that you believe he'll go straight now; but, if I gave him a pardon and he betrayed our confidence, we'd be the laughingstock of the mountains."

The Parson stood up, leaned over the governor's desk, and said, "Governor, there is just where the trouble lies! No one is willing to take a chance on these people. They are dying for someone to believe in them and love them." He let that soak in for a moment and then continued, "Sir, if you will grant Bill Henderson a full pardon, I personally will be responsible for his conduct. I am staking my ministry on that man. I will stand between Bill Henderson and the Commonwealth of Kentucky."

When Frakes had finished, the governor leaned back in his outsized office chair and considered the proposition that Frakes had just presented. Then rubbing his hands together as if to rid himself of any involvement, like Pilate with Jesus, he said, "Frakes, I believe you are a fool, but I'm going to do what you ask me to do." The pardon signed, it was sent to the county officials, and Bill Henderson was released, in due time.

The Parson had completed another milestone. But there was many a river to be crossed and many bridges of understanding yet to be built before his dream could truly emerge into reality.

6.

BLESSED ARE THE PEACEMAKERS

The mission project had been launched; but its success would take more than sponsorship, funds, dreams, and buildings. Something had to be done about the hatred that had been built up through the years in this isolated portion of Appalachia.

For example, Bill Henderson and Johnson Maiden had been feuding for years. It is hard to say where this feud —or any feud—began. Like spontaneous combustion, it just seemed to come from nowhere without any logical reason. But one thing was sure: Bill was carrying a gun for Johnson, and Johnson was carrying one for Bill.

Hiram Frakes believed that the One whom he served holds the answer to all fear and hatred. Since Bill Henderson was "king of the hill" in those parts, and since he had given the largest parcel of land for the Settlement, Frakes knew he was the key to the development and growth of radical change.

Strange as it may seem, Bill was a kind, gentle man to meet. He had a streak of decency in him, and was strongly inclined toward the Christian faith. He had simply been caught up in the code of the hills, which was "Do unto others before they do it to you."

Frakes, knowing that the Settlement could rise no higher than the thoughts and attitudes of its people, harbored a growing concern for Bill and the other feudists and bootleggers in the neighborhood.

Perhaps one of the reasons for the Henderson-Maiden feud was envy on Johnson Maiden's part. Bill had given his home place to the Parson and, as a consequence, had received quite a lot of attention. This special recognition of Bill, particularly since Johnson had no land to give, could have renewed old hatreds and brought the long-time feud to a fresh boiling point.

Whatever the reason for it, Frakes decided that he would make every possible effort to resolve the bitterness and hatred between the two men. Early one morning the Parson walked the three miles from his place to where Bill lived. As he walked along the trail, he prayed rhythmically with his steady gait, his shoes crunching the stones under his feet. "Oh, God," he repeated over and over, "help me in this meeting with Bill." For now he had the deep conviction that the future of his ministry in this place depended on Henderson's being converted.

As he approached the crest of the hill overlooking Bill's cabin, he saw the smoke ascending from the stone chimney into the clear morning sky. He knew Henderson was up. He sighed deeply as he realized the great importance of what he would say in the moments ahead. He had talked to Bill many times, but up until now he had always avoided the subject of Bill's feuds, as well as the feuding of the other families in the valley. This was the moment of truth! As he looked over the laurel-covered hills, he glanced skyward again and whispered, "Lord, I don't know what I'm going to do or say, but please help me, and help Bill Henderson too."

He knocked at the door, and Bill, with his trousers on but still barefoot, opened the door just a crack until he recognized the Parson. When he saw who it was he opened it wide and warmly invited him in. Bill was making coffee. He got out another cup, and they sat down by the morning fire. They talked about the weather, the crops, and made the usual small talk about conditions in the valley. As they were talking, Frakes's eyes scanned the wall and fell upon Bill's gun in a rack over the kitchen door.

For years this gun and others like it had been important adjuncts to mountain life. Guns were sheriff, judge, and jury. They were staff, compass, and guide. They determined the code, the philosophy, and the law. But just as Jesus once said, "The law says, but I say . . . ," the guns' days were numbered. Change was in the air.

Frakes's prayers, his faith, and his purpose (and his Lord) would supplant a new order for the old ways. A transformation was about to begin in those hills, for God was leading a man to do His work and His will.

"Bill," Frakes began, "you were carrying that gun the other day when I saw you going down the road. What for?"

Bill winced a little at this question, for he had great respect for this man. Then he drew himself together and boldly answered, "I was afraid I'd run into Johnson Maiden."

Frakes continued his questioning, "What would you have done if you had?"

"I'd have shot him," Bill replied without batting an eye, and without a moment's hesitation.

Now Frakes looked very straight at Bill, his blue eyes piercingly penetrating but warm. No, he hadn't forgotten that he was in the presence of one who had killed thirteen men by his own admission; but he was aware that this was a man who understood frank, straightforward language. Holding his eyes steady and measuring his words carefully, he said, "Bill, you're afraid of Johnson, and Johnson's afraid of you. The main thing wrong with each of you is fear of the other. If we could get that out of you both, this thing could be settled, I think."

Bill sat cross-legged on an old, handmade wooden stool. He'd been looking straight at the Parson as he spoke. His eyes now dropped to his big rough hands. He studied his broken fingernails thoughtfully and then glanced up at the gun over the door. Then, as if in objection to what the preacher had said, he said with emotion, "I ain't no coward, Parson, you should know that."

"Having fear and being a coward are two different

things," Frakes said, continuing his pointed reasoning. "I'll tell you what I want you to do, Bill. I want you to agree to meet Johnson Maiden in my presence and settle this matter in a Christian way. This will start to prove to these mountain people that there's no need of killing people to settle disputes. We've got to start somewhere, Bill, to make this community safe to live in. People respect you and will follow you. Will you do it?"

Bill reached over and took a piece of cold corn bread from a plate in the center of the table. He bit a sizable chunk off and chewed it slowly like a cud of tobacco. Swallowing hard, he said, "Parson, that's a big step you're askin' me to take. The Maidens have tormented me fer more than twenty years. They've burned my fences, killed my cattle, and, just a short while back, shot me through." His face flushed with anger fired by vivid memories of the past.

"But, Bill," Frakes persisted, "you've tried violence, and I ask you, has it settled anything? Are you better off? I'm your friend, Bill. You know that. Why don't you listen to me and try God's way for once?"

For the first time, Frakes saw the tension in Bill's face relax. As he now quietly pondered the last question, Bill's deep-set blue eyes moistened. Bill believed in God; but, as with many others, there was quite a disparity between what he really believed and the way he acted.

Raising himself off the three-legged stool and stretching to his full height, he said, "Parson, I been payin' a mind to what you been sayin'. It makes sense, I know . . ." And wrinkling his face in a distorted way as if the words he was about to say were sticking in his throat, he said with almost a groan, "I'll quit the feud if Johnson will—and no mountain man ever said quit before, thet I knows of."

Frakes rose to his feet, and a look of great relief crossed his face. He went over to Bill and put his arms around his great sagging shoulders. With tears in his eyes he said, "Bill, it was a great day when you gave sixty-eight acres of land for the church and school, but this is an even greater one. You'll never regret the step you've just taken."

The three miles home, for Frakes, was a victory march. It seemed as though his feet hardly touched the ground. God had answered his prayer. A new day was dawning for Henderson Settlement.

The next morning Frakes rose early and set out on another reconciliatory errand. This time it was to visit Johnson Maiden, for only half his job was done. As he passed Bill's house en route to Maiden's, he saw Bill limping out to meet him. The limp was a constant reminder of his hate campaign with the Maidens for they had put a slug into him a few months before and somehow the wound had never healed right. Frakes had a momentary qualm that Bill might have had second thoughts about their meeting yesterday, but it was very brief. Bill quickly dispelled it with the reassuring words, "Just you tell Johnson thet I'll stop feudin' if he will," he said in greeting. "I said I'd do it, and I will. He'll know that I'm as good as my word." Giving Frakes no time to reply, he hobbled back into his cabin.

When the Parson got to the Maiden cabin, he was glad that Johnson himself answered the door. The atmosphere was a little tense, for Johnson knew that Frakes and Bill were friendly. That meant to Johnson that Frakes was on Bill's side, because, in the mountains, you had to be on one side or the other. They did not allow for fence straddlers. But Johnson invited him in.

"Johnson," Frakes said, having decided to waste no time, "you were down to the mission store the other day carrying a gun. Is that right?"

Johnson nodded that he was.

"Why were you carrying that gun?" Frakes continued doggedly. "Were you going squirrel hunting?"

"No, sir," Johnson replied shyly with obvious embarrassment.

"Then why were you carrying it?"

"Now you've heered the reason already, Parson. Ye

know Bill Henderson and me hates each other. En I was afeered thet I'd run into him down there. I knowed he'd shoot me, if'n I didn't shoot him first."

"Do you know, Johnson, that's the very same thing Bill told me yesterday. It seems to me that there is nothing standing between you two men now but fear. Have you thought of that? I'm guessing you barely remember what your feud started over," Frakes countered.

"I reckon you're right," Johnson admitted sheepishly.

"Listen to me, Maiden. I talked to Bill yesterday, and he agreed to meet if you will, and settle this matter between you in a Christian way. I want you to go with me right now to Bill's house and make peace with him."

Johnson twitched nervously as he thought of the prospect. His system was so accustomed to the reaction of hate and fear that it could hardly adjust to the thought of "making peace" with anyone. After what seemed to Frakes a very long silence, Johnson finally responded with "Now, Parson, I don't want to go down there and get hurt."

"Nobody's going to get hurt if you do down there," Frakes assured him. "I'll stake my life and reputation on it."

Johnson got up, walked over to where Frakes was standing, and stared into his eyes for a few seconds as if to see some hidden meaning for this conversation. When he seemed satisfied that Frakes had no ulterior motives, he shuffled his shoulders as if to shake off the tension he felt and said, "Parson, I believe you're a good man. I trust you, and, while it's not the usual way we settle things here in the mountains, I guess it's worth a try."

Picking up his black tattered hat from the table loaded with dirty dishes and yesterday's food, he took a glance at his gun standing in the corner and said, "Let's go and see what happens."

Johnson was not a young man. The fight he had had to survive in these mountains and the years of hate and violence and killing had taken their toll. He seemed to be surveying his past as he walked by Frakes's side down to Henderson's cabin. Finally he began to try to express his thoughts. "Bill and I have had a heap of trouble through the years. We've done a heap of hatin' and fightin'. We're both agettin' on in years and it would be a good thing to make our peace before we hav'ta meet our Maker."

As they approached Bill's house, Johnson paused a moment to listen, in case this was a trap. Then he took a deep breath, put his head down and drew his shoulders tight, and walked on as if plodding through a snowstorm. He didn't look up until he was standing on Bill Henderson's porch.

Apparently Bill had been watching for the two men, for, as they started to call his name, the door opened, and he stood back to let the men enter. Frakes pushed in ahead. As he turned around, he saw the two avowed foes confronting each other eye to eye.

His heart began to pound a little. But Bill finally said, "Howdy, Johnson."

Johnson echoed, "Howdy, Bill."

For the first time in several hours, Frakes allowed the terrible weight to be lifted off his mind and soul. Here were Laurel Fork's worst enemies exchanging a friendly greeting—their first in many, many years. He knew their reconciliation was imminent.

Bill said, "Here, Parson, you take this rocker. Johnson, you and me can sit over h'yar on this bench." The two men sat side by side on the hand-hewn bench looking like bad schoolboys who had had to stay in after school.

Bill had been shelling corn, getting it ready for the gristmill and, to ease the tension, he continued his job. Johnson shifted his position a time or two and then picked up an ear and started to help.

Frakes watched the men for a moment and then said, "I'll bet that's not the first time you've shelled corn together."

This remark brought floods of old memories to the two men. They began talking and laughing about the days when they had romped and played in the fields and hills together as boys. There had been a day when they were "best" friends; and they exchanged several humorous episodes they had shared together, forgetting their hate-war of the past years.

When the atmosphere had become relaxed and completely congenial, the Parson broke into their reveries with, "Men, this is all most interesting; but we have come here today on serious business. You've just been talking about the fun of your childhood. Let's face the hate of your manhood. You've been feuding now for many years. You've caused family to fear family in this valley. Now, I'm asking you—both of you—to make your peace with each other complete as we sit here in the presence of God. I will be a witness to it. Then, together, we can show these mountain people that there is a better way to settle their differences than by fearing, hating, and killing."

Bill looked at Johnson and said, "Johnson, I ain't got nuthin' agin you, I guess."

Johnson swallowed hard and said, "Bill, I ain't got nuthin' agin you, I allow."

Those words were like a healing balm in that mountain cabin. Frakes could feel the pride and fear fade away. "Gentlemen," he said, "the Lord is in this place. Let's seal this wonderful moment with a prayer."

As the Parson knelt by the ancient cane-bottom chair, he began his prayer for these two rough, hate-ravaged men. As his eyes were sometimes open during that prayer, he was able to see Johnson and Bill kneeling together at the old bench as humbly as two little children. Each had his face covered with his hands, as if to shut out the guilt of the past. Tears flowed down Frakes's face as he thanked God for this "greatest miracle" and prayed as he'd never prayed before. When he had said "Amen," he embraced Johnson and Henderson as two brothers. "This is a great day for the people of the mountains," he said. "Let's have a peace dinner at the church next Sunday."

They shook hands all around and agreed.

On the next Sunday, Bill, dressed in his Sunday best, walked into the little chapel with five of his crony-feudists. He was followed by Johnson Maiden and six of his former henchmen. It was a sight to be remembered! Here, worshiping together, were two men who a few days before had been carrying guns and pure hatred for each other.

It was time for the service to start. Mabel, Bill's twelve-year-old daughter, was the Sunday school and church pianist. Bill, rarely a church-attender, had never heard her play. The hymn was announced: "What a Friend We Have in Jesus." As Mabel went to the piano, sat down, and began to play, big tears welled up in the proud father's eyes. Pulling out his red bandana handkerchief, he blew his nose and wiped the tears from his face. All the people were touched to see this big man—so very tough, they had thought—moved in tender emotion.

At the close of the service Bill went to the front and shook the Parson's hand. He said, "Preacher, I guess you seen me acryin' like a kid during the service; but when I saw my little girl playin' the piano and lookin' like an angel, my heart felt like it would bust. When I remembered how mean I've bin and how patient you and the Lord has bin with us, it's almost too much to understand. And then, there she was, playin' so pretty."

After everyone had spoken to the Parson, the two factions of the old feud sat down to eat the "peace dinner." The Parson sat at the head of the long table with Bill and his clan on his left and Maiden and his men on his right. That was more than a dinner; it was a sacrament, in which two enemy clans sealed the covenant made the week before when the three men knelt in Bill's modest cabin. And it was made for life! They had buried the three things that had created conflict between persons: envy, fear, and pride. And the good Lord had done the rest.

7.

TRAIL'S END FOR BILL HENDERSON

Christ said: "They that take the sword shall perish with the sword" (Matthew 26:52). That statement could be paraphrased to say: "He that takes a gun shall perish with a gun," and the mountain people were aware of this law. The wailing of a widow en route to the cemetery to bury her husband who had been shot was a common sound in these hills. Death stalked the mountain trails, and a somber realization rested on every mountain man that he might be the next to die.

But the Parson had brought new hope to the children. The first school dormitory, made of logs and containing five or six bunks, was used to house children who had been orphaned or who lived too far to walk to school. Buses were impractical since the roads were too rough. The jagged rocks soon tore up the tires or broke the springs of a motor vehicle.

Mabel Henderson, Bill Henderson's pretty and talented little girl, stayed at the dormitory rather than walk the muddy, rough, and rocky three miles to the Settlement school every day. When Saturday rolled around, Mabel was granted the privilege of going home for the weekend.

One Saturday morning the shrill cry rang through Partin Hall, "Mabel's getting ready to go home!" The girls all knew what this meant to Mabel, and while possibly a little envious they were glad she was close enough so she could go home. Jenny, Mabel's closest friend, looked out at the sunny day and smiled at the other girls as she said, "Look at her, she can hardly wait."

Mountain children love their parents and their homes,

no matter how poor and unkempt. But it seemed that Mabel loved her parents more than most. And it was obvious to all who knew the Henderson family that Mabel was the "apple of her daddy's eye" and she adored him. Her daddy's life of hardship and suffering had only endeared him to her all the more. To Mabel he was no outlaw. He merely lived by the law that had been etched in the minds and hearts of mountain men, and on the stocks of their guns. They really hadn't deliberately broken the Ten Commandments. They just had never thought of them as having something to do with their lives. True, the mountain preachers proclaimed the Gospel the best they knew; but it is doubtful if many of them, being illiterate themselves, stressed the personal ethic "Thou shalt do no murder."

Anyway, to the mountain men there was a big difference between murder as such and "killing." Murder was taking life without a cause; but killing was just "giving a man his just due." It was justice mountain style, and, as they themselves would say, "You couldn't fault that."

Now Mabel Henderson, scrubbed clean, rosy-cheeked, and in her freshly ironed pinafore dress, waved to the other girls in the dorm kitchen as she skipped down the path leading to the road that would take her home. "Goodbye, y'all!" she yelled. "See you tomorrow at church."

"Did you ever see anyone so happy to be going home?" one of the girls in the kitchen asked, speaking to no one in particular.

As Mabel glided happily along the road toward her cabin home, it seemed to her that the birds sang more joyfully than usual. The colors of wild flowers making their first appearance of the season seemed a little more vivid than ever before. It was April, and the warm sun was beckoning all nature to quit its winter sleep and rise again. Little shoots of grass peeked through the soil softened by the spring rains. A jonquil poked its slender leaves heavenward as if to wave timidly at the happy lass skipping down the trail.

The little girl's heart beat high with joy and excitement. There were so many things to tell about school: the plans for Commencement, which was something very new; her good grades; her new pinafore—and she would be able to show them how she was learning to sew, for she was wearing her first finished creation. Oh, there were so many good morsels of news that she was anxious to share with her mother and father.

Her young legs, unaccustomed to walking so fast, were growing weary as she climbed the last hill before reaching home. As she stood for a moment looking down on her home place, she had the feeling that things didn't seem quite normal. Her father, usually at work in his garden on warm days like this, was not to be seen. Could he be ill? Yes, something was wrong down there!

As her heart began to beat wildly in fear, she heard one of the neighbor girls calling, "Mabel, Mabel! Wait a minute."

Breathlessly the girl approached her and blurted out, "Mabel, yer dad's been killed! Marion Overton just shot him!"

Mabel wouldn't believe her ears. It couldn't be true. No, no, it was a terrible mistake. Her daddy couldn't be dead.

Terror shot through her frail body and she felt too weak to go further. Then her face reddened with childish rage, and she ran toward home as fast as her feet would carry her. She would prove the girl's words were false!

As she rounded the cabin, the tragic truth unfolded before her. Her father lay where he had fallen. His head was pillowed on the old black felt hat that he had always worn out-of-doors, and his arms were folded across his breast.

"He knew he were a-dyin'," sobbed her twelve-year-old brother Edward, who was standing at his father's feet.

"He stretched himself out, and I heerd him say a prayer, and . . . and then he went."

Shaken by shock and almost stricken dumb by her sudden grief, Mabel ran and threw her arms around Edward and, hugging him close to her, sobbed, "Where's Mama?"

Edward began to cry more loudly with the question, and Mabel, sensing there was still more to be told, pushed him from her to scan his face. When she saw the terror and pain written there, she shook him, saying, "Edward, tell me now, where's Mama?"

Edward could hardly form the words, but finally he managed to say between great sobs, "She's gone."

"Gone!" Mabel repeated hysterically as the tears began to stream down her face, "gone where?"

"I dunno'," Edward sobbed again. Then seeing Mabel's incredible look of near collapse, he tried to go on to tell her the horrible happenings of the last hour or so. He ended by saying, "Anyways, I heerd Marion tell her he'd shoot her too 'lessen she left here quick. I reckon she's halfways up the holler by now," the shaken boy stammered.

Mabel couldn't believe it. She couldn't accept the idea that possibly her mother was gone too. Her mother and father were dearer to her than life itself. She *had* to believe her father had been killed, for there he was on the ground; but she could not believe she had lost her mother too.

Suddenly she started to run toward the hill back of the house. She would find her mother. She must find her mother. With tears blinding her vision, and beside herself with grief, she took the wrong trail. She stumbled dumbly along the narrow path until her sister Lonnie came and found her and brought her back to the empty cabin. Had a young girl ever been called upon to suffer so much grief in such a short span of time?

News travels fast in the hills, and soon neighbors and kin folk began to gather at the Henderson home. Little by little the whole tragic story was pieced together.

TRAIL'S END FOR BILL HENDERSON

Bill Henderson and Otis Ellis, his daughter Ruth's husband, were getting ready to plant potatoes in the garden. The ground had been prepared, and they were resting for a few minutes near the barn. Hiram Rufus and Wilburn, Bill's two sons, were playing nearby. Marion Overton, Bill's stepson, came down the hill from his house and started an argument with Otis. There had been some family dispute about the division of Bill's property among the children. Marion was demanding more than the others would get, and Bill kept repeating, "All my children are a-goin' to share exactly alike." There was the usual accusation and denial, then the sharp report of a pistol. Killings happen fast in the mountains, usually on the tip-end of an argument or at the edge of an obscene name.

Bill said to Marion, "Don't shoot Ellis. He hain't done nary a harm."

At that, Marion turned his gun on Bill and fired.

Bill, bending over in pain, yelled, "Don't shoot agin! You've killed me."

By this time Marion was like a stalking animal in his insane rage. He picked Bill up, stood him on his feet, and fired three more shots into his body. Bill fell, mortally wounded but still conscious. He had often said that he wanted to die with his boots on, and it seemed ironic that his request had been granted.

Bill knew he was dying, but through force of habit he reached for his old hat and slowly crunched it into a pillow and tucked it under his head. He prayed the prayer that Rufus had mentioned and folded his arms across his chest and went to meet his God.

As the neighbors nearby heard the shot and started to gather, wild confusion followed. The murderer ran through the house and up the hill, but no one followed in pursuit. By the time it dawned on everyone what had happened, he was probably two miles away.

Bill died as he had lived—by a gun! His gun with its thirteen notches was not even used in self-defense. Since

Bill was a changed man, there is considerable doubt that he would have used it if he could have.

The last Sunday of Bill's life on earth he had given a Christian testimony at the church service at Henderson Settlement. Stepping to the front of the little chapel, with faltering words he said, "Hit's borne in on me like I ort to testify here and now, fer hit might be my last chanct. I'm feelin' proud to tell y'all 'at I've made my peace with Almighty God, and thar hain't nothin' atween me an' my Lord."

They were prophetic, those words "Hit might be my last chanct," for it was. But that testimony rang in the ears of those attending the service that night, and they knew that Bill Henderson was a changed man. This man who they all knew had killed thirteen men in his life had found a new forgiveness—and God!

Three days later Bill Henderson took his last ride. Not erect in the saddle saying "Howdy" to fellow mountain folk, as was his custom in life; but in death, with a haunting smile on his face as if he were saying, "I've found peace at last." Now he was free of all the feuding, the hate, the rigors of mountain life in Laurel Fork.

Parson Frakes had lost a good friend; but right now he had to face the fact that there might be friends and relatives of Bill's out for revenge. This had always been the unwritten code of the mountains. These next days could be crucial to Laurel Fork. With a heavy heart, he thought about slipping away into Pineville and turning the service for Bill over to the mountain preachers. It would have been the easy way, and he was very, very tired, as he had suffered a severe loss in Bill's death.

But Frakes was really never one to run from divine duty. His temptation was tempered with the knowledge that the mountain folk have their ways and perhaps it would be best to let them pursue their ancient drama of death.

When he was first called to preach, the word of the

Lord had come to him: "Preach the preaching I bid thee preach." But still came the recurring thought that perhaps the mountain preachers could handle this delicate situation better. As he sought guidance in the matter, the words of Scripture came to him. "Who knoweth but that thou art come to the kingdom for such a time as this?"

Out of his terrific inner struggle came this chastened answer to God, "You've helped me so far in these hills, and I know you'll lead me on." Putting an end to his soul's conflict, he added these submissive words, "I'll do what you want me to do."

The church was filled for Bill's funeral. After his own daughters along with the glee club from the Settlement school sang "Jesus, Lover of My Soul," Frakes stepped to the foot of Bill's coffin, took his small Testament from his pocket, and read slowly and impressively the third chapter of James. Then with deep feeling he began to speak: "My friends, we are here to commit the body of William Henderson to the earth and his soul to God. We all know how swift was his summons. But we know too that he died with a prayer on his lips, and we are willing to stake our lives on God hearing that prayer. I am not here to pronounce a eulogy over this man, who was my friend. Yet I must mention the fact that over and over again since this tragedy men have said to me: 'Bill Henderson was a good neighbor. He had a kind heart.'

"I shall never forget one Sunday morning at the Settlement when Bill saw his daughter Mabel at the piano for the first time. As he heard her play the hymns of the church, tears ran down his bronzed cheeks. He was unashamed of those tears, being the man he was. At the close of the service he said to me, 'Parson, we're kind of an uncivilized lot, quarreling and fighting like we do; but my daughter Mabel here is gonna' be different.' He seemed happy at the thought that one day things would change.

"But, my friends, it is not of the dead I would speak today, but of us who remain. What will be our reaction to this tragedy? Shall we choose revenge and blighting hate? Or shall we be brave enough and big enough in our souls to see the better way, the way that makes for peace? 'Vengeance is mine, I will repay, saith the Lord.'"

Then fondling the little New Testament, he again quoted from James: "The tongue is a fire, a world of iniquity. . . . It defileth the body and setteth on fire the course of nature, and is set on fire of hell. . . . It is an unruly evil, full of deadly poison." He then said, "Words are weapons that kill, and God is the only conqueror of our temper and our tongues."

A few people squirmed nervously, realizing that even a preacher is not immune from mountain revenge, and they were astounded by Frakes's courage in trying to come to grips with the issue surrounding Bill Henderson's death.

The wind swept softly through the maple trees in the churchyard as the Parson paused and scanned his audience. Then he continued, "What is true courage? Is it to follow our feelings, our natural emotions? Does it mean to follow the line of least resistance, to give vent to our hatred and anger? Or is true courage to dare to follow the One who died upon the cross for our sins that we might learn to conquer hate through love? I have had to wrestle with hate in my own life, but I'm telling you that I have found through the grace of God we can conquer it, and learn the lessons of love."

The sobbing so common at a mountain funeral ceased. Under the stately, swaying hemlocks God's message was going home, healing, strengthening, curing the hatreds of the hills.

Even Bill's own son-in-law Otis, who, according to his own words, was "hot with wrath inside," said, "I reckon now I can hold my peace."

That funeral sermon set the pace for the years ahead. Its truth will echo in the hearts of all those present for time to come. The Parson had dared to step out, as he had many times before, on the empty void, only to find the Solid Rock beneath.

Bill Henderson was dead. But his death occasioned a spiritual flame which still burns in those hills to this very day. "He being dead, yet speaketh."

8.

LAW AND GRACE

Frakes was a great believer in the Scripture, "The law came by Moses, but grace and truth came by Jesus Christ." Grace came first; but the law had its place too. Although Frakes was a kind, gracious man by nature, when toughness was required, he combined grace with grit and was fearless; he was filled with righteous indignation when an occasion required drastic action.

Revivals, or protracted meetings, were a regular spiritual diet at the Settlement. They served a twofold purpose. First, they gave the people something to do in the evenings besides drinking and fighting. And second, they channeled grace into the hearts of the people, creating an antidote for lawlessness and mischief. For Frakes, it was as simple as that. From the first he had concocted an effective blend of a saving and a social gospel. In fact, he considered the two one and the same. He fed the hungry, but he had the conviction that feeding them was without purpose if you let them starve in their souls. He gave them clothes; but what was clothing if underneath a new coat beat a heart full of violence and murder!

So he pounded away at both souls and bodies, mending, healing, and ameliorating. For Frakes, every part of his work was an exciting challenge, and he relished every minute of it. It was like a chess game in which real, living men were the pawns; and, by the grace of God, he as the player prayerfully moved and maneuvered them toward a kind of spiritual victory. Other people could live in Middlesboro and Pineville and play the games of making money, seeking pleasure, or enduring boredom; but

LAW AND GRACE

Frakes had found his niche in the foggy little valley of Laurel Fork and was one of the happiest men in the world.

A happening took place on a quiet Wednesday night during one of the revivals at the Settlement. The people had come down through the twisting trails, some singing on their way, the children carrying their shoes to save them, and most of them with their kerosene lanterns for the return trip. The tabernacle (an improvised auditorium) was filled with men, women, and children. They were dressed comfortably, the men in their bibbed blue jeans, some with miner's caps with the little clamp above the bill to hold their carbine lanterns, which they would use instead of kerosene ones for the return trip in the darkness. The women wore their calico dresses, and the children the clothing they had gotten from the clothes barrels at the "store." Little Mandy, who was twelve years old and in the first grade, drew special attention with her very outdated, high-laced, pointed shoes. She especially loved them because the high heels made nice "clicking" sounds when she walked on wooden floors. Mandy thought the shoes were beautiful, but they drew snickers from the boys, who thought they looked unusually funny. Perhaps Mandy was a premature "hippie," with her high boots and long, stringy blonde hair. Anyway, she was dressed for a special occasion, and a revival was just that!

The men sat in the rear where they could stretch out, doze if they wished, and carry on a whispering conversation if the sermon got a little long or boresome. Going to church for these mountain people was as much a social occasion as a religious one. Saint and sinner went, but for different reasons. Life for these people was a notch behind the early American pioneers, and they had no telephones, television, electricity, moving picture shows, etc.—nothing except their favorite pastimes of eating, talking, and going to church. And for some, going to church was the best of all. The best singers in the valley were there with their guitars, and there was foot-tapping singing when little Mable Henderson played the piano and the congregation joined in one of their favorites, like "When the Roll Is Called up Yonder."

No, going to church was not just for the religious, as in city churches. Everyone went. It was the only thing to do, and the preacher knew that both the best and the worst in the community were present. His sermon had to be a combination of food for the saints and fuel for the sinners, as he stoked the furnaces of hell and warned the lost of their plight without God. And this they liked. These mountain people, saved or lost, believed the Bible from "kivver to kivver," and they had no time for a preacher who didn't load both barrels of the Gospel gun, fill it up with razor blades and gunpowder, and fire pointblank at the audience.

On this particular night, the evangelist, a mountain preacher, was pouring it on with all his might and main when a man walked down the aisle, leaned over, and whispered to Frakes, "There's trouble outside."

"What kind of trouble?" whispered Frakes.

"Our deputy sheriff is drunk and is about to shoot a man."

Frakes sat in the pew a moment trying to decide what to do. He knew that murders happen fast in the mountains, and that liquor had a part in about three out of every four of them. He also knew the deputy was a dangerous man when he was drunk.

Deputy Sheriffs were hard to come by in the remote section of Laurel Fork. For one thing, they didn't enjoy too much longevity. These mountain folk, descendants of Scottish and English highlanders, were an independent lot. They brooked no interference from outsiders, and Frakes, by birth, was not one of them. His life was on the line every day, and he was a living example of Christ's words, "He that loseth his life for my sake shall find it." He had to walk a fine line between caution and courage, and between kindness and firmness, and above everything else he had to be sure he always projected fairness. This he did with uncanny ability.

The deputies chosen by the high sheriff were often a

sorry lot—men who were often looked upon askance by their own neighbors. So like all other law officers they were considered enemies of the populace. Besides being the kind of men they were, they represented authority; and the *law* was loathed becaused it interrupted the natural ebb and flow of life in the valley. After all, if a man wanted to wipe out an enemy, whose business was it? Freedom to many of the mountain people meant the freedom to kill, to maim, and to eliminate their enemies.

With the "invitation" going full speed ahead and several mourners at the altar, Frakes eased out of his pew into the aisle and walked softly on tiptoe back to the door. As he stepped outside, he saw the deputy standing by a young man with his 45 caliber pistol sticking into his chest. An old-timer at the door warned Frakes, "Don't go out there, Preacher, ye'll get shot. That deputy is as drunk as a fool."

But Frakes always figured that David was right when he said, "One can chase a thousand, and two can put ten thousand to flight." Either God was with him, or he was not; and if he was not, the Parson shouldn't be in Laurel Fork in the first place.

Frakes slipped out in the shadows and approached the quarreling pair from the rear. Tapping the deputy on the shoulder, he said, "Tommy, give me that gun!"

Now the moment of truth had come. Would the deputy react kindly to this intrusion, or would he turn the gun on Frakes? The future of Henderson Settlement was wrapped up in the answer to that question.

Tommy, shaken by the daring of the Parson, mumbled with his thick tongue, "Is that you, Mr. Frakes?"

"You know who it is, Tommy. Give me that gun!"

Being caught off guard by Frakes's sudden appearance, Tommy became submissive and handed over the gun like an obedient child.

Frakes took the deputy by the arm, led him aside to the sheltering boughs of a big tree, and began to talk softly to him, "Tommy, I've stood by you. You're the only law officer we have here in Laurel Fork. What got into you? What has the boy done to make you pull a gun on him. Surely, not something bad enough for you to kill him."

"I guess I don't rightly know, Preacher. I s'pose I've had a little too much to drink. But, one thing, I never did like that kid. He acts too big for his britches."

"What did he ever do to you?" Frakes queried.

"I ain't aknowin' exactly; I just don't like him."

At that moment the young man whom Tommy had threatened to kill walked up with a friend he had enlisted to help. "Need any help?" the boys asked.

"No, I've already got all the help I need," Frakes said, as he pointed upward.

At that, Tommy lunged at Frakes, "Give me that gun, I want to kill this kid."

Frakes, seeing that the deputy's mind was inflamed with liquor, said to the boys, "Go get my car! I see we've got a trip to make to Middlesboro."

With the help of the two boys they got the reluctant Tommy into the car, and the four men headed for Middlesboro with one boy on each side of Tommy holding him down.

When they were passing Tommy's house, he yelled at Frakes, "Stop at my house for a minute. There's something I gotta' do."

Frakes said, "I'm afraid there's nothing you've gotta' do now, Tommy, but go to Middlesboro with us."

After they had driven on a couple of miles, Tommy said, "I wanted to get someone to go on my bond."

"What's that?" Frakes asked.

Tommy, almost weeping now, and totally subdued, said, "I wanted to git someone to go on my bond."

"I'll do that myself, when the time comes," Frakes said consolingly and drove on.

The deputy fell into a drunken stupor on the long, hazardous trip down the rough mountain road. When they finally reached the highway, the drunken Tommy awakened and began to pray: "O Lord, bless Mr. Frakes; he is a righteous man."

Instinctively the poor man knew that Frakes was doing him a favor by keeping him from killing an innocent man. And although he didn't enjoy the idea of being taken to jail, Tommy obviously was having second thoughts about his activities of the evening. He knew jail was the lesser of two evils. He offered no resistance from that time on.

When Frakes unloaded him at the jail he said to the high sheriff, "Here's one of your law officers. He's given us a lot of trouble tonight, but he's your problem now. I'm going home and get some sleep."

On the next Sunday morning the people were gathered in front of the church, as they do in the mountains, waiting for Sunday school to begin. They glanced down the road to see a nicely dressed family coming toward the church. Of all people in the world, it was Tommy the deputy and his family!

Tommy walked past the people with their curious stares and straight up to Frakes, who was standing in the door. "I want to see you for a minute, Preacher," he said.

Frakes, not knowing quite what to expect, took him inside and gently patted him on the back, as if to say, "Bygones are bygones. We're friends again."

Tommy reached for Frakes's hand and clasped it tightly as he said, "Preacher, I want to thank you for what you did for me last Wednesday night. You kept me from killin' that kid. I told the high sheriff [who had taken away Tommy's authority and his badge] that if he'd let me go, I'd swear off drinkin' and become a Christian citizen. And I mean to do that this mornin' with your help and God's. As you see, I brung my family with me to church this mornin,' and I mean to be doin' that from now on."

As Tommy and his family sat in church that morning, Frakes could see the leaven of the Gospel working again in Laurel Fork. He humbly bowed his head and thanked God for His guiding hand of protection and grace! Everyone there that morning knew that God was at work; for only God could bring about such a change of heart in a man like Tommy.

The choir sang more lustily than usual:

> Grace, grace, God's grace;
> Grace that is greater than all our sin.

As they sang, Frakes—a very tenderhearted man— wiped a tear from his eye.

Tommy became a pillar in the church of God and kept his promise faithfully through the years.

9.

THE MOONSHINE MACHINE

When Frakes first went to Laurel Fork, every man in those hills was gainfully employed making moonshine. He asked one of the men one day, "Will you tell me if you know of a single man in this community who is not making moonshine, or who never did make it?"

The man, lowering his head a little, said, "No, sir, I don't know of a man in these parts who doesn't make 'shine including myself."

Prohibition was still in effect, and any kind of liquor was in great demand by both the rich and the poor. But the Settlement 'shiners had an elite clientele. They sold their liquor to many of the "top" people—to the county, state, and federal officials whose duty it was to keep the law. These people in Pineville, Middlesboro, and as far south as Knoxville felt safe in dealing with the Laurel Fork mountain people, for they knew they were tight-lipped. The code of the hills was speak softly, be gentlemanly, carry a gun, and never betray a trust. So even many federal officials charged with arresting and prosecuting violators of the Volstead Act went to the mountains for their liquid refreshments. They bought it there for two reasons, it was the best moonshine in the area, and thy knew their purchases would be a well-guarded secret.

The moonshiners had a good business going; for they sold to some of the judges, district attorneys, United States Commissioners, and high officials of the railroad companies. Because the Laurel Fork folk knew of the hypocrisy of these officials, they really got "riled" up when someone tried to interrupt their moonshining business.

FIRE IN THE HILLS

A classic story of the "feds" and the moonshiners probably originated in these hills, for it was notoriously dangerous for the revenuers to crack down on these mountain people who brooked no disturbance of their illegal business.

The story goes this way: One day a federal officer came out to scrounge around, smoke out some of the moonshiners, and destroy their stills. He met a little boy about ten years old and asked, "Son, do you happen to know where there are some moonshine stills?" The boy looked knowingly at the officer.

"I'll give you a dollar if you take me to one," the officer bargained.

That was good money for a mountain boy, so he said, "Okay, you go right down that path to the bottom of the hill, and when you get to the creek, turn right. It's right in that thicket you'll see there, about fifty yards away."

The revenue officer thanked the boy and started to walk down the path as he had been directed. The little boy followed him saying, "Come on now, keep your bargain. Give me my dollar."

The officer, in a hurry to pursue the still, said, "I'll give it to you when I get back."

"No, sir!" The boy demanded, "I'll take it right now, 'cause you ain't comin' back."

When Frakes was trying to collect his hundred acres of land—the amount he thought would be adequate for a school, church, and campus for the Settlement—he discovered a beautiful site. It was eleven acres of rolling land overlooking the valley. He was told that this land belonged to a man who lived five miles down the valley. One day he mounted his mule and rode the five miles over the rocky road to see the man about the land. Frakes arrived late in the afternoon and was told by the woman at the cabin that her husband wasn't home, but if the Parson would just make himself comfortable on the front porch, he should be home soon.

THE MOONSHINE MACHINE

As Frakes sat on the little porch, he noticed a small clearing of land of about half an acre with a picket fence around it. The rest of the property was unfenced yard, trees, and wilderness. He saw that a little path led from the cabin to the clearing, which he thought was the garden, and on around to the far side. Three pickets had been removed from the fence to allow people to pass through. As he was surveying the situation, he saw a young boy about twelve years of age walking up the wilderness path to the fenced plot. But when the boy reached the fence, he skirted around the opening in the pickets and went directly to the rear door, where he and his mother carried on a whispered conversation. They were standing where the boy could gaze on Frakes suspiciously as they whispered. When they had finished their secret conversation, the boy ducked back down the path, around the picket fence, and then on down the path toward the thicket. It all seemed very strange and unusual to Frakes.

What had happened was this. The father and his son had been tending their moonshine still and had started up the path for supper. When they saw Frakes, dressed in store clothes, sitting on the porch, they thought he might possibly be a federal officer. The mother told Frakes later that she had told her boy, "Tell your pappy it ain't nobody but a Methodist preacher, so come right on. It's all right."

Though Methodist preachers were rare in those parts, the people had heard of Frakes, as his reputation was well known in the valley. They invited him to stay for supper and he accepted. After the meal they built up a warm fire in the fireplace and sat around and talked. Long into the night Frakes related his dream and vision for the people of the valley. He told the little family of four—there was a daughter younger than the boy—circled around the fire about his deep desire to build a school for the children, a church where all the families of the area might worship and pray and sing together, and a community house where there would be planned recreation.

The two children were especially excited as he talked

about a school built on the plan of city schools (which they had never seen), with factory-made desks, store-bought books for every pupil, and a furnace to keep the children warm in the winter. Their little black eyes danced in anticipation of all the things that might be in their future. Since they had never seen a real school or church, it was all beyond their fondest imagination; but it sounded wonderful as they tried to visualize it all.

Frakes talked of employment for the men, and told the children about films he would someday show them of real live people walking and talking on a screen. He talked about special entertainment on Saturday nights for all the people with folk games and fun for everyone. Then he approached the subject of his need for their eleven acres with the knoll overlooking the entire valley. It was on its summit that he wanted to build the school and the church. He told them honestly that he had no money and no promise of any in the future; that his collateral was his faith in God and his belief in a better life for the mountain people.

It was very late when they finished talking, so they offered him their extra mattress made of corn shucks, which was on the floor of a lean-to connected to the cabin. There was no heat, but Frakes had grown accustomed to mountain accommodations and accepted it gladly.

Long after he had gone to bed, he heard voices in the main room. For a while he thought perhaps this couple might still suspect him of being a revenuer or the like, and might be plotting to do him in. Apprehensively he got up and put his ear to a crack in the wall. Then he heard the man say, "Nobody's ever keerd for our kids afore. I wants them to hev' a better chance then I've hed, so I guess if there's a glimmer of hope we ort to hep."

That was sufficient for Frakes. His suspicions quelled, he drew the heavy quilted blanket up over him and nestled down in the shuck bed to sleep soundly until daylight.

The next morning as the men were waiting for the corn bread and grits, the moonshiner told Frakes that if he was who he said he was, and if he was going to do what he promised, they would deed the eleven acres to the Methodist church.

It was upon that land that the modern school was finally built, and it was to that sacred hill that hundreds and thousands of children would go to learn readin', ritin', 'rithmetic, and religion. These were Frakes's four R's; and though the Christian religion might have been last in the curriculum, it was not least.

It seemed that something wonderful happened to everyone who gave land to the Settlement, and these people were no exception. The moonshiner, a gifted man in many ways, gave up his moonshining shortly after that visit, moved to the Settlement, and became Frakes's farm manager. He served honorably in that capacity for several years.

The ten-year-old girl graduated from the Settlement high school, worked in Frakes's office, and became assistant matron in the girls' dormitory. Other children born to this family received the benefits of their parents' generous gift too. That gift amounted to the sum total of a new life for each member of that family. "Bread cast upon the waters shall return after many days."

10.

FOR OF SUCH IS THE KINGDOM OF HEAVEN

Children were the chief commodity of the little community of Henderson Settlement and of all Appalachia. Within a radius of five miles there were more than 1,200 children. Frakes longed to adopt them all and take them into his big, growing family. But of course this was humanly and financially impossible. Urgent need, however, always found him ready to accept another challenge with compassion and understanding. It seemed that Providence had bestowed upon him that Lincoln-like gift of handling people with diplomacy and concern.

One morning while the Parson was eating breakfast cooked by his "girls" in the dormitory kitchen, there was a knock at the kitchen door. Frakes left the big table and went to answer it. Standing in front of him was a lean mountain man twisting his dilapidated black hat in his hands. Nervously and self-consciously he presented his case.

"Parson, I've heerd of you and the fine way you're helping our children in these parts. Up where I live, about three and a half miles from here, are two little girls living with their mother, and, I must say, they are in a poor plight.

"Their daddy, who was my own blood brother, was killed in a mountain feud about eight year ago, and their mother and them live in a shaky little shack. They make a little 'shine so as to eat, and stuff like that there. Them kids has never been to school er had any larnin'. And all they know is what they hear around a place where men gather to buy liquor, an' thet ain't good.

"Now their mama has been indicted for moonshining, and fer some other things I'd rather not speak of, and I'm afeerd she's agoin' to be sent to federal prison. These here girls, Wilma and Gladys, is only nine and 'leven years old. They is alarnin' to cuss like troopers, and it looks like mebbie in a couple of years they're agoin' to get in real trouble, 'cause some of them there men has already got their eyes on them.

"Now, Parson," he went on, "whut I come here fer is to ask ya if theer be any way we kin git 'em in here at this here place. If something hain't done purty soon, Wilma and Gladys 'er goners. Do ya' know whut I mean?"

Frakes did know what Bill Sowder meant, but his mind went quickly to the crowded conditions of the dormitory and the school. He could realistically visualize the work and patience it would take to orient these neglected girls to the high standards of Settlement living. He considered the lack of funds and what adding two more hungry mouths to the already crowded table would mean. Yes, he evaluated the situation carefully and came to the conclusion it was impossible to admit the girls. But he looked at the concerned, haggard-looking man who had a desperate need, and throwing caution to the wind, said, "Sure, we'll take them. That's what we're here for."

The mountaineer heaved a deep sigh of relief, exclaiming, "Thank the good Lord—and thank you, sir!" It seemed that having the heavy tensions relieved now allowed him to stand a little straighter. Putting the old battered hat on his uncombed head, he anxiously asked, "When do ya want me ta fetch 'em?"

Thoroughly involved now, Frakes said, "Bring them as soon as you can. The sooner they come to the Settlement, the better off they'll be."

Three days later Bill Sowder jerked the rein on his old bony donkey as he pulled into the road leading up the

slope to the dormitory. "Git up, Jenny!" he begged as he
prodded the old mule up the hill.

Jenny, with great difficulty, dug her hoofs in to fetch
her heavy load up the steep incline, a feat that had
stalled many a Model T Ford. It was hard, even for
dependable Jenny, because not only was Bill astraddle
her, but also the two girls and their two big cardboard
boxes of belongings as well.

Frakes heard the ruckus and left his office in the dormitory to go out and help them up the hill. When he saw
the situation, he said, "How about you girls jumping off
so the mule can make it up the hill?"

Gladys, the eleven-year-old, flicked her dress up care-
lessly like a true tomboy, spat out a mouthful of tobacco
juice, and jumped off Jenny's back. "I'm Gladys," she
said to Frakes with a toothless smile.

Frakes responded to her greeting with an affable shake
of his head, noting that she looked like some humorous
character from a country medicine show.

Wilma climbed down in a little more ladylike fashion,
but put her hand out as she had seen the men do at her
saloon-home. Shaking Frakes's hand, she said, "You'll
have to 'scuse my sister Gladys. She ain't got much
larnin'."

Looking at Wilma as he greeted her, Frakes noticed
that she also had a mouthful of tobacco. With all that she
had a pretty face, freckled and pert. Her reddish hair was
neatly combed but the "washline" that circled her face
showed that it had been some time since the girl had had
a good scrubbing.

Unkempt and untrained as these two little waifs were,
Frakes fell in love with them immediately. Behind the
masks woven by neglect, hardship, and barbarous living,
he could see the prospect of two beautiful and poised
young women, who would some day be a credit to Laurel
Fork and Henderson Settlement. The mischievous gleam
in Gladys' eyes and the radiant smile on Wilma's face
were, despite the girls' tobacco chewing and liberal use

of "cuss" words, the harbingers of promised charm and femininity. Fortunately for the Settlement, Frakes had an uncanny talent for looking beyond the rough exterior and seeing, by faith, what miracles a few weeks in a warm, friendly atmosphere could do for a personality. Just so, in his mind's eye he saw these two hopeless-appearing girls in a transformed condition.

Wilma and Gladys had learned to fend for themselves. Reared in the confines of a mountain cabin saloon and bootlegging establishment, they knew how to fight, to scratch, and to pour out verbal obscenities and profanities at the drop of a hat.

On the first day of school when a dispute arose on the playground, Gladys kicked a boy in the groin, jabbing her sharp elbow in his face at the same time. This sent the boy, with wounded pride as well as body, running to the teacher. Although he was much larger and probably stronger than Gladys, he felt no embarrassment in airing his grievances to his understanding teacher. For he had already learned the rule that was to prevail: No fighting on the playground.

The teacher immediately sent for Gladys and, when the girl arrived, proceeded to inform her that discipline was not meted out by the children at the Settlement. She ended her little session with Gladys by saying, "From now on, if there's any discipline to be given, it will be administered only by your teachers or your principal. We want to make sure that injustices will always be handled in a fair and just manner."

Upset by these new, strange rules Gladys retorted, "Well, where I come from, it's every man fer hisself; I'm used ta taking keer of myself; but—" Seeing her defense was not going over so well, she added, "But I'll try to do it yur way. I'm warning ya', though, they'd better not push me too fer!"

For a few days it looked like Frakes had gotten a little more than he had bargained for with Wilma and Gladys, especially Gladys. For one thing, she couldn't understand why she was not allowed to chew "tobaccy" in school; and she had difficulty in keeping the "damns" and "hells" and a few other unmentionable words out of even the most casual conversation. Thankfully, every day saw little glimmers of progress, as these girls—illiterate as high-landers from the remotest mountains in Asia—began to adjust slowly to their new environment.

The girls thrived on the good food and the clean beds. The bathtub was a special delight to both of them; so much so that they had to be allotted so many minutes for their baths, else the other girls would not get their turn. The matron wished many times that it were as easy to clean up the girls' minds as their bodies.

The first time Wilma and Gladys sat down at the long dining table with the other children, they started to grab their food and gulp it down before grace was said. They were told kindly by the matron that at the Settlement they were all aware that a benevolent God provided their daily food, and as civilized people they believed they should thank Him for it. Fortunately, the two girls took instruction in stride and accepted it as one of the prices to be paid for having such a wonderful, clean new home. They learned quickly both to wait for the blessing and even to say it. Gladys' first prayer was a classic. It went something like this: "God, we'uns thanks ya for this here food you done gave us. It shore is nice of ya, away up in heaven, to 'member us poor folks away down h'yar on this earth. We're mighty proud to be h'yar at this here Settlement, and I asks ya ta' please let us live h'yar from now on. Amen."

Since neither Wilma nor Gladys had ever attended school, they had to start in the first grade. They realized quickly that they were far behind the other children their ages; so they worked hard to make up. The first year they finished two grades; and like the boy Jesus "increased in wisdom, and in stature, and in favor with God and man."

Like so many of the mountain children, Wilma and Gladys possessed good singing voices; and in the evening when the children gathered around the piano to sing with Miss Lambdon, their voices rose above the others like a skylark over a sparrow. The transformation had begun. Wilma and Gladys were blossoming, along with scores of other children at the Settlement, into lovely, mannerly, thoughtful children. The influence of the Settlement was good.

Frakes's old-fashioned objective was for every one of his charges to be introduced personally to the Savior. He let it be known that the decision of accepting Christ as Lord must always be personal, sacred, and without coercion or pressure; but like a skilled magician he used indirection to introduce the magic, wonderful powers of Christ.

Though no pious saint, he endeavored to practice Christianity in every detail at the Settlement, and he believed that Christianity should be more seen than heard. Invariably the children were attracted to his Savior, and, ultimately, each in his own time and way made an open confession of his faith.

For Wilma and Gladys it happened on a warm spring evening at the Settlement log chapel. The windows had been opened for the service, and the pungent smell of April was in the soft night air. Childish voices lifted in praise to the Savior wafted out over the low hills of the valley:

> Praise Him, praise Him,
> Tell of His excellent greatness,
> Praise Him, praise Him,
> Ever in joyful song.

That night Frakes talked on the subject of praise. His text was, "The heavens declare the glory of God, and the firmament showeth his handiwork."

"These words," he said, "were written by the psalmist David. David lived in hill country much like the country we live in here at the Settlement. Above those hills where David lived towered Mount Zion, the mountain of the

Lord. So David said, 'I will look unto the hills from whence cometh my strength.' The secret of David's strength was his trust in the Lord. Because of it he was able to subdue bears, lions, and, eventually, the giant Goliath.

"David was an expert on giving praise to God not only with his lips, but also by his life-attitudes and his actions. He also believed that all nature praised God. In the words of our text he is saying: 'The heavens declare the glory of God, and the firmament showeth his handiwork.' Like a conductor urging on a great symphony orchestra, David says, 'Come on, stars, come on, moon, come on, sun, come on, clouds! Let us all declare the glory of God!' Then he turns to the firmament—the earth—and says, 'Come on, sea, come on, mountains, come on, trees, come on, you beautiful flowers, come on, fields of waving grain, come on! Let everything that God has given life upon this earth, let us all praise the Lord!' And you know, they have been doing that down through the centuries. All nature praises the Lord and declares his glory!

"But man should praise the Lord too. I don't mean just saying Praise the Lord with your lips. I mean declaring God's glory by acknowledging him in your hearts and lives. Have you done this? Are you doing this?

"Well, if you have not, I'm going to ask you to begin praising the Lord with your life tonight."

As the invitation song was sung, "Just as I am, without one plea," little Wilma walked forward and knelt at the altar of the log chapel. Two or three girls who had already received Christ stepped forward and knelt beside her. Then Gladys, dressed in a new white frock and with her long reddish hair flowing down her back, pushed her way through the crowded pew and joined Wilma at the altar. Frakes, sensitive man that he was, wiped a tear from his eye as he knelt by these two mountain girls and prayed with emotion for their salvation. It was truly a night to be remembered.

To Frakes, this was a climactic culmination of all the social and educational efforts they had all put forth—the establishment of a working relationship between a person and God. This was missions; this was his real mission! His greatest joy was in leading his charges to follow the One who had called him to this work, Jesus Christ.

The story of Wilma and Gladys could be repeated a hundred times or more in the experience of Parson Frakes. From the Settlement have gone physicians, teachers, military leaders, businessmen, nurses, ministers, and home-makers—all made from the same cloth as these two girls.

Gladys and Wilma went on to let their lives count! They became active in the choir, the school glee club, the Sunbonnet Quartette, and the 4-H Club. At a statewide meeting of the 4-H Club, Wilma was elected state secretary. It was a long jump from the cabin-saloon and a mother who had been indicted and convicted for various crimes. But by the grace of God and the help of the Parson, they made it.

11.

FROM WHISKEY TO WHEAT

Many people have difficulty with the miracle of Christ turning the water into wine, but Frakes never once doubted the miracle. At the Settlement he had seen feuding changed to faith, profanity changed to praise, disorder changed to order, and lawless people changed to law-abiding citizens. It was safe to say that he had more fun than any preacher for miles around, for he was where the action was.

When he saw the last vestiges of moonshining disappearing from the valley, another problem loomed on the horizon. Many of the men had been lifelong moonshiners. Now, they were faced with the question of how to make a living for their families. Many of them found work in the mines; but not all of them. Something had to be done to feed the one thousand mouths of Laurel Fork valley.

One day, while pondering the situation, the Parson went for a walk. He walked until he stood on the summit of the hill overlooking Laurel Fork. From this point he could see for over a mile to the east, as far north as the big forest, and nearly a mile to the south. The ground, though rolling, was tillable. True, it had grown up in scrub brush, for during the moonshining era there was just no interest in nor time for farming. The men were too busy making and selling their 'shine. As he surveyed the acres of unused land, an idea began to emerge.

Immediately on his return to the Settlement, he went into Pineville and sought out the county agricultural agent. Frakes pointed out the details of his plan. He said, "There are more than seven thousand acres not being used in Laurel Fork. Why couldn't we raise some grain out there?"

The agent answered him by saying that all it took to grow wheat were workers, seed, land, and machinery.

"Well, we've got the people and the land," Frakes said excitedly. "Now, we've got to see about that seed and machinery." The idea he had had that morning was feasible, he had now found out happily; so he put legs and muscle to it so it might materialize.

Bread was indeed the staff of life for the people in the valley; and if the uncultivated fields could be made productive with wheat it would save the mountain people from being destitute, or having to go elsewhere for work.

The Red Cross furnished the seed—180 bushels of the finest wheat seed money could buy. The Campbell brothers, who operated a large farm near Colmar, Kentucky, heard of the proposed project and the need; and they offered the services of a threshing machine—free of charge. Cradles for harvesting could be made in the Settlement blacksmith shop; and the county agent had consented to provide a drill for planting.

Early in the fall the big threshing machine was delivered to the Settlement by the Campbell brothers. The mountain people turned out to see the strange and wonderful sight. The Parson had his staff ready to sign up all the farmers who would be willing to undertake a wheat crop. There was excitement in the air, as wheat had never been grown in that area; and nine tenths of the people had never even seen wheat growing.

For the next few weeks, there was the sound of a "going" in Laurel Fork. Mules worked overtime—as did the men who drove them—clearing the fallow ground and dragging sled loads of rocks out of the fields. When all was in readiness, they drilled the wheat with the machine which the genial county agent, R. V. Trosper, had loaned them.

By early October, scores of acres had been planted with wheat. The Settlement farm itself had five acres of wheat. This was very little by Kansas standards, but it was a healthy token of future farm prospects in the valley.

Over one hundred mountain farmers planted wheat that fall.

Through the winter and spring, nature worked overtime to do her part for the Laurel Fork wheat crop. After the deep snows had thawed in March, the green wheat poked through the lush, virgin mountain soil, and gave promise of a bumper crop. The mountain people watched it grow with keen interest, and its daily progress became a prime topic of conversation.

In May, it was knee high; and in June, waist high. In early July, the warm summer sun turned the green stalks to golden yellow; and the time of harvest was at hand. The first wheat threshing in Laurel Fork, ever, took place on July 4. Frakes called it a new "independence day" for the people.

The big threshing machine was rigged up, and mule-drawn wagons brought the wheat to the schoolgrounds for the threshing. The ladies prepared a big dinner for all the threshers; and mountain eyes were wide with wonder as the golden grain began to flow into the grain sacks. The yield was a healthy twenty to twenty-five bushels per acre, excellent for that part of Kentucky, and the quality rivaled the best that Kansas could grow.

Before the harvest Frakes was in Middlesboro displaying wheat as tall as a man; and the city folk agreed it was the finest they had ever seen in the Tri-State section. Frakes was quick to point out that all the wheat did not measure up to the tremendous proportions of his sample; but that enough would be grown to furnish bread that winter to hundreds of families. Pellagra, a skin disease, was prominent in the Laurel Fork section; and doctors said that it was caused by a deficiency of protein. A gristmill was installed at the Settlement; and the new grain, in due time, would be ground to make whole wheat bread, which is high in protein.

Wagons and sleds were used to haul the grain by the more than one hundred farmers who had grown wheat the first year. The Settlement threshed the wheat without toll, or charge, and the farmers were proud as punch as they loaded the big sacks of freshly threshed grain on their sleds and wagons. Some left part of it at the Settlement "wheat storage house" to be ground later. The wheat they took home with them was ground in their hand gristmills to be made into bread and cakes.

As Frakes watched the busy mountaineers carrying grain instead of toting whiskey, he thought of the other transformations at the Settlement. He remembered that just a few weeks previously over sixty-five men of those hills, members of the Community Improvement League (most of them former moonshiners), had met in the tabernacle. In gratitude for the transformation of their valley, and for the better life they were enjoying, they presented the Parson with a beautiful Bible. He felt the fact that he had eaten, slept, and lived with these people, no matter what their circumstances, had paid big dividends. Like Moses he had chosen "rather to suffer affliction with the people of God, than to enjoy the pleasures of sin for a season; Esteeming the reproach of Christ greater riches than the treasures of Egypt: for he had respect unto the recompense of the reward" (Hebrews 11:25-26).

There was scarcely a mountain home in all the valley where he had not spent the night and shared the personal problems of the family. Though, by their standards, "a "furriner," he had been accepted as one of them; and that was the greatest compliment they could pay a person.

Yes, it seemed only a few years; but truly he had already become a legend in Laurel Fork. In fact, when the postal department decided to put a post office at the Settlement, the people without a moment's hesitation, decided it should be called "Frakes"! So Frakes, Kentucky, became a symbol of hope in those mountains. People came from far and near to see what "God had wrought"; and they were not disappointed.

He had seen a mail route where there had been none. He had instituted medical services, with a registered nurse, where formerly people had been without medical attention altogether. They had not even had a hypodermic needle to ease their pain as they were dying. He had seen moonshining all but disappear from the valley. He had seen fathers engaged in gainful and honorable employment —in the mines, in the fields, or on the railroad six miles away at Chenoa. The Settlement itself had been able to employ more than twenty-five men regularly; thus, they had become intimate associates in his missionary endeavors. He had seen the income of the little valley jump from less than $15,000 for all the 150 families with each family averaging about $100 a year, to nearly $150,000 per year. He had seen feuding halted. He had seen the school attendance grow from thirteen in that first log cabin school to nearly four hundred students, coming from all over the valley.

During his tenure at the Settlement, he had seen more than 800 students cared for in the dormitory. At least 2,000 boys and girls had attended their school; 94 had graduated from high school, and 54 had gone on to college. Many of these had received degrees, and some had even gone on to do postgraduate work. Several had received their master's degrees and had taken a significant place in society, some at the Settlement school itself. Frakes knew he had much to be grateful for, but the end was not yet. His active mind could not rest as long as there was an uneducated, disenfranchised child in that valley. So he continued to dream big dreams, and he planned his work and worked his plans.

What he would do next, no one knew; but the folk of the community knew that, whatever it was, it would move Laurel Fork forward. As a matter of fact, Frakes was beginning to look beyond the circumference of this area for other places with like needs. He felt that the Settlement people were almost to the place where they could help others now, and, to be truly oriented to this new way of life, they must do just that. That was what his work was about and, he believed, was the gist of being a Christian. But there was still work to be done.

12.

THE GOSPEL ACCORDING TO
BLOODHOUNDS

To imply as perhaps we have that Laurel Fork was heaven on earth would be to make a gross misrepresentation of the facts. The Parson had his enemies, and some of the mountain men still pursued the life they had always known, in spite of all the changes around them. Those that still favored "moonshining," naturally looked at Frakes with a suspicious eye and never quite accepted him. They felt security in doing the thing they knew best, and were determined that no preacher " 'er furriner" was going to change their way of life. Their attitude created an occupational hazard. Because they persisted in breaking the law, the law was always a threat to them, and Frakes along with it. They knew he stood for law and order and, right or wrong, they didn't like him. To a few, he was still a "nosy intruder" and one to be watched.

Lige, the thin-as-a-rail moonshiner, was busy at his still. He smiled as he saw the golden stuff winding through the coils and flowing into the brown jugs he had lined up around the still. His partner in the illicit operation was busily working at his side, as Lige announced, "Hit'll make at least ninety gallons of the finest moonshine thet's ever tickled a mortal tongue, I reckon."

"And Old Doc and Stoney, over in Middlesboro, tole me yest'idy thet they had their $700 in cash all riddy fer us," his partner said jubilantly. "Thet is, if'n we kin deliver ninety gallons to thim afore this weekend."

As the two moonshiners watched gleefully, their prize batch of 'shine flowed musically into their prepared containers. They could almost visualize now that $700 in their hands and how good it would feel; but their joyful reverie was interrupted by an audible rustling in the thicket near their clearing. Lige automatically reached for his shotgun; but before he could get to it, a voice called out to him:

"Hold it, Lige, we've got the goods on you this time, and we will take care of all that whiskey you have made. There's been a long dry spell, and this dry ground's been needing the real good shower it's going to get!"

Two federal deputies from Pineville had them cold. The jig was up, the party was over! As the deputies entered their little hideaway and approached Lige with their handcuffs, Si, seeing they hadn't noticed him yet, darted from the clearing and ran away.

The deputies shot at him; but the shot only accelerated his pace. He ran for the woods, and was probably a mile away before they got the cuffs on Lige.

Lige knew he was caught red-handed and there was no way out, so he begged to be allowed to say good-bye to his family. This was the usual request and the deputies customarily honored it; so they headed for Lige's cabin.

Susie, Lige's little ten-year-old girl, had heard the deputy's car drive up in front of the cabin, so she opened the door to see who was coming to visit. Visitors to the mountain people were always a special treat. When she saw her daddy getting out of the car with handcuffs on, she let out a shrill scream of sudden fright and then began crying uncontrollably. The other children, alerted by Susie's scream, quickly started trooping in to see the cause of her alarm. The boys had been chopping wood in the back, and the younger ones had been playing in their self-made playhouse in the garden. Lige's wife had been baking bread, and she came running with her hands covered with flour. When they saw Lige, they all stopped as if frozen in their tracks. They waited for the explanation that was bound to come. Of course, all of them knew of Lige's secret vocation.

THE GOSPEL ACCORDING TO BLOODHOUNDS

Lige went up to his white-faced, frail-looking wife, who stood wiping her hands on her big blue printed apron. She kept wiping them, as if to wipe this whole scene away; but instead, Lige made it more real as he said to her, "I reckon I'm fair caught this time. I shore hate to leave you'uns fer I knows hit'll be a hard winter fer ya'." Then speaking to the boys, he said, "I want you'uns to take keer of yor ma and the little ones. Ya' heer me?"

The boys nodded affirmatively that they did. With that, Lige picked up the littlest child, who was just able to toddle about, and kissed his undernourished cheek. A tear fell to the ground as he leaned over to put the child down. Without looking back, and with his head bent with grief, he went out and got into the deputy's car for the trip to town.

Lige spent the night in the Pineville County jail; but his term was short, for his cronies bailed him out the next day.

Lige had had an old moonshining partner named Tim Creech. Tim had "seen the light," had given up moonshining and drinking, and had been hired by the Parson as the Settlement teamster. Since quitting Lige and liquor-making, Tim had tried to pay up his old bills, so he had had a hard time financially. Consequently, he and his big family had continued to live in their little one-room cabin which was hardly large enough for two people. All summer long the family had sweltered from the heat because of the confinement of their quarters. The Settlement folks, knowing their predicament, got together and built them a brand new house. To the Creech family it was a mansion, and they were looking forward to moving day, and were grateful for the tremendous labor of love of their friends.

Early on Sunday morning, the day after Lige and Si had been discovered by the deputies of Pineville, Tim's new house had ignited and had burned to the ground. It happened in that darkest-before-dawn hour when no one is up, so there was no opportunity to save it. Tim and his family were heartbroken.

The Parson was immediately suspicious about the fire, but he remained tight-lipped as usual. He didn't say a word to anyone, but everyone knew that the Parson, who was a stickler for the law, wasn't going to accept this "burnin'" as accidental.

Old Joe Cox tells about the incident in mountain language. "Come to think of it, I reckon the Sky Pilot [Joe's name for Frakes] didn't jest *happen* to be at the Settlement when Tim's house burned. I'm a-guessin' that Providence took a hand in it and seed to it thet he was right thar. Now everyone in Laurel Fork knowed thet Tim's house belonged ta the Settlement.

"Well, I seed the Sky Pilot a-goin' down the road on Big Jim—thet's thet old mule no one dares ta fool with exceptin' the Sky Pilot—and by the set of his jaw I were shore sartin there were the devil to pay.

"Long 'bout noon he done cum back, and less'n an hour atter that 'long come the sheriff a-holdin' some of the ugliest critters I ever did see in all me born days. Bloodhounds, he called 'em. I followed 'em down to whur thet new house hed bin, and whur they was nuthin' now but a big ole pile o' ashes. I'm a-tellin' ya they wuz a heap o' folks down there by now; an' they wuz all plum scared.

"Well sir, them bloodhounds sniffed 'round aplenty in them thar ashes. And thin they streaked it down the creek en' went straight ter Sam Tuttle's place. Everybuddy knowed thet Sam wuz sorter a pardner to Lige en his moonshinin', and thet he bootlegged the stuff considerable 'round these h'yar parts. But when them thar dogs crossed the creek an' nosed along up that thar cove to Si Hignite's cabin, I wuz plum flabbergasted.

Si wuz a-sittin' on his ole porch, 'en would ya' believe that thet thar dog went up thar and laid hisself right down aside ole Si. As we'uns stood thar a-watchin', I sez right out public like, 'Well, I'll be jiggered! If'n I hed as sweet a gal and boy as Si's got, I swear I'd risk hell afore I'd do a mean trick like thet thar to the Settlement, whut were aimin' to give my younguns a right smart larnin', and were bringin' them up in the fear uv the Almighty God.' Yes sir, I sez them very pinted words afore I had time to think, I did.

"Yer askin' whut us mountain folks is a-aimin' ta do 'bout this h'yar shame whut's a-drug onto us? Wall sir, I'm on the shady side of seventy, and my rumantics hez mighty nigh ruint me fer work; but I'll be goldarned if'n I ain't ready to jine in a house-raisin' for Tim and the Sky Pilot soon's as I kin git trees down out o' thet tall timber.

"We're a powerful backward lot, we air, way up h'yar in these rough hills, but I vow I got sense enough and decency enough under these h'yar blue jeans ter stick by a man like the Sky Pilot. He come up h'yar ter help us en ter learn our children to quit a-quarlin' en' a-killin', an' to live honest en peaceablelike."

And at this point, out came old Uncle Joe's red bandana from the cavernous hip pocket. He jabbed at the tears that persisted in appearing and said in a half-whisper, "I'll be durned if'n I keer who sees me a-cryin'. I've shore got my reasons."

So Si was arrested, both for bootlegging and for arson, and taken into town immediately. Typically, his buddies tried to bail him out, but the judge, this time, set the bail beyond their means.

Frakes didn't believe in meddling much with the affairs of the local citizenry. He felt that bootlegging was a matter for the law to deal with, and he usually left it in their hands. But burning down people's houses, to his way of thinking, was going a bit too far. There wasn't anything private about that. His action (and on the sacred Lord's day) did more to create respect for the law throughout the entire community than a hundred sermons. Laurel Fork approved of "the Gospel according to bloodhounds."

43.

THE SUNBONNET GIRLS

The Parson, in his own way, was a promoter par excellence. While he was not trained to be a public relations man, he possessed the natural gifts that would have made him a Madison Avenue genius if his calling had been in that direction. He had a keen sense of appropriateness mixed with a generous amount of "ham," and those ingredients came in handy on many occasions.

To accompany him on his missionary trips, he took the quartette of teen-age girls that he had organized and named the "Sunbonnet Girls." Their singing ability was secondary to their appearance, for they set the stage, in their sunbonnets, calico dresses, and pink gingham aprons, for the message he wanted to present. When you take four natural-looking teen-age girls, attired in native mountain costumes, and stand them up before an audience with their bright smiles and tuneful voices, what more can you need? They captivated audiences wherever they went, and were a perfect prelude for Frakes's introduction of his mountain work.

One of the quartette's most extensive trips was one through the West in 1941, which took them into sixteen states. They made sixty-one appearances in churches, clubs, and conferences. So demanding was this eight-thousand-mile journey that each girl had to have two uniforms—one for wear, and one for repair. They appeared at such exclusive churches as the Vine Street Methodist Church of Hollywood and the Crescent Heights Methodist Church of Beverly Hills. The music director of the Crescent Heights Church was the man who wrote the musical score for the movie *Snow White and the Seven Dwarfs*. So, you see, they were in good musical company.

The girls' main qualifications were their youthful exuberance and their native love for singing. Though they had few formal practice sessions, due to their regular school duties, they sang incessantly around the dormitory. Their housemother, Mrs. Julia Colson, reported once to Mr. Frakes, "There's surely no lack for music in our dormitory when the Sunbonnet Girls are around."

When the girls packed their bags and started on their Western trip in the Settlement car, none of them dreamed of the extensive adventure in store for them. Geography came alive for them as they journeyed across the vast expanse of the Western United States. The Grand Canyon of Arizona, which had been just a name in a geography book, became vividly the "biggest ditch in the world." As the Sunbonnet Girls stood on the rim of the Canyon and sang "Farther Along," the reality of just how far that was became more meaningful to them, and both life and song took on a new dimension. When they visited the Painted Desert of Utah and Arizona, with its pinkish red soil and its lush carpet of blooming flowers, they marveled at the skill of the Master Painter, who had given nature its rich hues, its purple sunsets and golden sunrises.

For one of the girls, Alcatraz Island was the wonder of the world, with its giant spider-web of buildings sprawling on a tiny spit of sand in San Francisco Bay. Still another girl thought the Golden Gate Bridge, with its massive expanse of steel interwoven into a giant arch, and thrown across the Bay by the genius of man, was the highlight of the trip. Another girl considered the giant redwoods, which were old when Christ was born, as the greatest sight she saw on the eventful trip.

For the Parson the greatest thrill of all was the six thousand Methodist delegates from all over the world who heard the girls sing. Their enthusiastic ovation and reception of the group was a heartwarming joy indelibly imprinted on his heart. After his years of struggle and sacrifice, he was being paid by the good Lord in the coin of heaven for his faithfulness to His service.

Probably a highlight of the trip for the entire group was their visit to a real-for-sure ranch in San Mateo. A family of good Methodist people owned the twenty-room ranch house with its hundreds of broad acres. They turned the key of their luxurious home over to Mr. and Mrs. Frakes and the girls so they might have a good rest before they took off again on their strenuous journey.

During their stay at the ranch, they all enjoyed the heated swimming pool, the tennis courts, a shooting gallery, a bowling alley, and the sumptuous meals prepared by the ranch's professional cooks, as well as the service of real butlers.

Talk about "The Beverly Hillbillies!" With the owners gone and the run of the ranch given over to them, they really enjoyed themselves. They had come a long way from Laurel Fork, with its simple, backward ways, but the Sunbonnet Girls, encouraged by the Parson and his zest for living, made the transition easily. It was a most enjoyable holiday and a memorable experience.

Best of all, through the more than sixty contacts on this Western trip (which was only one of many that Frakes made through the years), many new friends were made for Henderson Settlement's growth and future. Many more prayers would be going up for the work daily.

After more than eight weeks on the road and 10,000 miles, it was a weary sixsome that made its way eastward after their last engagement in Illinois. As they crossed the Ohio River into Kentucky, one of the girls yelled out, "Stop the car! Stop the car!"

The Parson, looking around and seeing that the girl didn't look ill, asked, "Why? What is the matter?"

"Oh, Mr. Frakes, I just want to get out and kiss that good ole Kentucky dirt," the Sunbonnet Girl replied.

The Grand Canyon had been grand, the Golden Gate Bridge golden, and the redwood trees big; but to these girls, born in the hills, there was no place like their old Kentucky home.

It was the Parson's perseverance that kept the work going at the Settlement. His "line had gone out through all the earth," and communications with the prayer partners throughout Methodism was the lifeline of the Settlement. He used every device at his command to contact his constituency. Every year WLW, the radio station in Cincinnati, Ohio, gave the Parson and his Sunbonnet Quartette free time on the first Sunday in February. Many churches in five states put radios in their churches and Sunday schools to hear the program. Then they took an offering for the Settlement. This annual event brought in thousands of dollars for the school and the work, and added greatly to the growing list of interested friends.

While the Settlement was never underwritten by the Methodist Church per se, Frakes was given *carte blanche* entry into every corner of Methodism. He and his quartette appeared regularly at the state annual conferences, and even the General Convocations, such as the one held in San Francisco. Parson Frakes's story was exciting and productive, well presented and true; and the people responded in kind to his consecrated work. The girls and the Parson were also featured on the popular radio program "We, the People."

While his bank account never showed much of a surplus, there always seemed to be enough, when notes came due, to meet the immediate obligations. It was like Elijah and the widow's cruse of oil—never too much, and never too little, just enough to make ends meet.

Building was added to building, by faith; and it wasn't long until 24 buildings could be counted. Project was added to project, and like Topsy in *Uncle Tom's Cabin,* the work just "growed" and flourished as though some heavenly angels were helping it along.

Many needs came with the growth, but these were filled quite naturally and without overdue strain. As Frakes stood outside the dormitory one moonlit night (few things were comparable to those hills splashed with moonlight under a starlit sky) and heard the Sunbonnet Girls at an impromptu practice singing, "He'll understand and say, 'Well done,'" his mind flashed back across the years.

First, there was the big decision to leave the city church and the opportunity to climb to the top in Methodism. Then there were the years spent in gaining the confidence of the mountain folk. It took nearly five years of eating, sleeping, and living among the folk of Laurel Fork before they really believed in him and accepted him. And there were the years of hard work, sweat, and tears—the years of building and rebuilding. There were the long, arduous trips to raise money to feed the hundreds of mouths, to hire teachers and to get accreditation for the school and to build goodwill and interest in the project.

Now the seed—the good seed—had been planted; and he was beginning to see signs of a golden harvest. Already some of his graduates had gotten their degrees from college, and were back teaching at the Settlement. This was the fulfillment of one of his fondest dreams. There were prospects, and good ones, that a new road would be built within the next two years. Everything seemed to be flowering out according to the original plan, and he felt deep gratitude in his heart for the "works of God."

Some of his brethren had gone on to large urban churches, and were receiving large salaries, along with great prestige and influence. But the Parson stood on that grassy knoll in the moonlight and heard the melody of his girls being wafted out on the soft night air:

> Cheer up, my brother, live in the sunshine;
> We'll understand it all by and by.

He felt a tremendous satisfaction. He wouldn't have traded places with a bishop, or even the President of the United States. He had a deep sense of "knowing why he had been born"; he knew his purpose in life, and he knew where he was going. Did any multimillionaire have more?

14.

THERE'S LIFE IN THOSE HILLS

From the start the Settlement project was news-worthy, and, happily, its news was almost all good news —in contrast to the headlines formerly made by the kill-ings, moonshining, and violence of the area. In Frakes's carefully prepared journal entitled *Kentucky Mountain Missions, 1925-1963,* there are countless articles from periodicals near and far. Thousands of words—yes, tens of thousands—have been written about the work of the Settlement. The *Christian Advocate,* the *Reader's Digest, Coronet* magazine, and many others covered the absorb-ing story of the growth of the Settlement at Laurel Fork.

But the crowning honor came on September 15, 1941, when *Life* magazine came with its writers and photog-raphers to cover a mountain wedding. They could not have picked a finer couple to write about, or a more beautiful setting, or a more favorable season. The wedding came at the start of summer, when the fields were green after the spring rains, the flowers were in full bloom, and summer's magic was at its peak.

Gilbert Dove, a young farmer from Elnora, Indiana, had heard of the fine work being done among the moun-tain people of eastern Kentucky. He felt "led" to go down and lend a hand in the building and expansion. Gilbert was experienced in maintenance, and he fit perfectly into the Settlement picture, serving as electrician and service man.

Dove was a bachelor, having been too occupied with his large farm in Indiana to do any courting. There was something about the setting at Laurel Fork, something about the laurel and rhododendron, about the clear moonlight nights, about the wild isolation of the place that made a man (or a woman, for that matter) feel romantic.

In making his service rounds, Gilbert kept stumbling onto Hazel Petrey. Hazel was the first girl to graduate from the Settlement school and was now the assistant matron of the girl's dormitory. She was a lithe, shapely, blue-eyed brunette with olive complexion and rosy cheeks, typical of the Anglo-Saxon stock of these hills. She could well have come from the Scottish Highlands.

Gilbert was not altogether unfamiliar with attractive girls. He had attended Asbury College, in Northern Kentucky, and had met his share of winsome, beautiful girls. But romance has its own time to come to life, to bloom, and to flower, and it seemed fate had planned for Gilbert and Hazel to meet each other in these fertile hills, and to judge each other far superior to anyone they had ever met. And that is the way it was.

"Where's the main switch box, Miss Petrey?" Gilbert asked, on visiting the dormitory one day.

He actually knew where it was, but some way had to be devised for him to make a more personal contact with this girl. He already was beginning to have strange feelings about her.

Swinging her body in a right turn, with her attractive homemade calico apron swirling like the skirt of a Spanish dancer, she said, "Right this way, Mr. Dove."

She led him to a dark closet, turned on the pullchain light, and pointed to the switch box.

"You look powerful pretty under that light," Gilbert ventured, his voice trembling a little, for he knew he had beguiled her into this situation.

"Thank you, Mr. Dove, that's very flattering," Hazel answered coyly.

With that, Gilbert put his arm around her waist and tried to draw her closer to him.

Hazel wiggled out of his grasp tantalizingly, and said,

THE
PHOTO
ALBUM

Bill Henderson

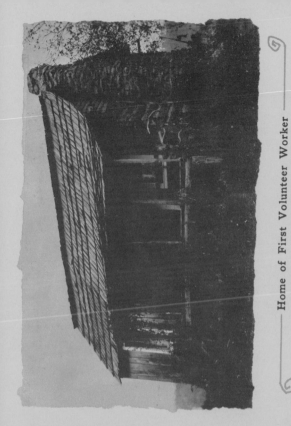

Home of First Volunteer Worker

Uncle Scott Partin

Mountaineer at His Hand Grist Mill

First New School Building

Opening Day at New School

Bishop Henderson at Abandoned Moonshine Still

Visit to the White House (left to right): W?, and J?(?),
Mabel Henderson, Mrs. Frakes, President Herbert Hoover,
Hiram Frakes, Ethel Bowlin, Margie Bowlin, Elmer Partin

Hiram Frakes, the postmaster of Frakes, Kentucky

Boys and Girls in the Settlement Dormitory

Parson Frakes at the Entrance to Henderson Settlement

Out of the Ashes—A New Partin Hall

Wedding of Hazel Petry and Gilbert Dove

— W. E. Cissna Directs a "Singing Game" —

Men's Banquet at the Settlement

Mabel Henderson in Her Classroom

They Came to Learn

Parson Frakes, the Rev. Lewis Nichols, and the Sunbonnet Girls

"Why, Mr. Dove! I thought it was the switch box you were interested in." Then, with a sly smile on her face, she teasingly said, "I'll see you later, Mr. Dove." With this she hurried away and left him alone in the closet with his switch box.

Well, that's the way it began. It wasn't long before the word got around that Gilbert and Hazel were courting. This was always a choice morsel of information in that secluded community, for interesting news was hard to come by.

Finally Gilbert and Hazel were seen together openly, walking down the road by the church in the evening, holding hands, and acting like the real lovers they were. They sat together in church, and it was no longer a secret to anyone that Hazel and Gilbert were serious about each other. The girls in the dormitory often whispered about them as they did the dishes. Their innocent gossip was very exciting to them, for Hazel and Gilbert were an interesting topic. Love is always intriguing when the participants are attractive, wholesome, and well matched. Groups at school often talked about the two during lunch hour; and knowing laughter often attended their conversation.

One night at dinner, Gilbert stood up and addressed the group around the table, "Hey, everyone," he said, "I've got an announcement to make. On June 15, Hazel and I are going to be married . . . at the Germany Church."

The dormitory crowd broke out in happy applause. They all approved and had been waiting for such a statement. It seemed the fitting and final chapter for a mountain girl, who, undernourished and illiterate had come to the Settlement, and through her own efforts and the help of the dedicated staff, had risen above her environment. She had studied hard to get her high school diploma, and she was now serving the Settlement well. She was deeply respected, for she had become a person of transparent, sterling character. The announcement of her engagement was a high moment for everyone.

FIRE IN THE HILLS

*

Life magazine had been contemplating doing a piece on a mountain wedding for a long time. Frakes had been in correspondence with them ever since they had heard about his work through the *Reader's Digest* articles.

When Hazel and Gilbert announced their plans for a wedding, Frakes got a note off to Joe Clark immediately. He told the *Life* photographer about the forthcoming marriage and suggested it just might be the one they would want to cover. The *Life* staff considered his offer and decided to do the story.

The church at Germany was a mission-extension of Henderson Settlement. It was located in a picturesque little cove, surrounded by rhododendron and mountain laurel, six miles down the road from the Settlement.

On the morning of June 15, the poorly maintained road was alive with activity. Mules, horses, wagons, and people afoot made their way back and forth preparing for the big moment for Hazel and Gilbert. They wanted everything to be perfect; after all, it wasn't every day that a major magazine covered an event in these remote hills. Although most of the people had never even seen a copy of *Life* magazine, they had a vague idea what it was like; and they knew one thing—it was important.

The little log church was decorated as it had never been decorated before. The girls from the dorm, along with the adult staff members, spent the "wee" hours of the morning gathering laurel and rhododendron and wild mountain flowers and carried them to the church by the armful. Carefully and lovingly, they placed sprays over the windows and doors, at the end of the pews, and around the pulpit until it was a solid mass of greenery splashed with the purple and pink of the mountain blooms. If they had hired a professional decorator, the scene couldn't have been more lovely. It was a masterpiece of decorating art fit for *Life*, or *Look*, or any other national magazine.

THERE'S LIFE IN THOSE HILLS

The weatherman cooperated for the gala event. It was a typical nice June day, the air balmy and filled with the soft sweet scent of wildflowers. At 9 A.M. the people began to gather. Mountain people, because they have plenty of leisure time, usually go early to church or to any other public event. They like to see the crowd gather, greet old friends, and make an occasion out of any kind of meeting. By ten o'clock the church was filled to capacity. *Life* magazine's crew of photographers and network of wires and lights gave the event an aura of excitement never before seen by the native people. Flashbulbs went off for an hour or more before the wedding procession started, with the mountain people blinking their eyes and shielding their faces with their hands, trying to keep out the glare of the bright lights.

In typical mountain style, a preaching service preceded the wedding ceremonies. While the wedding was to be at high noon, the preaching service began a little after ten o'clock. The Rev. W. E. Cissna, the pastor of the Henderson Settlement church, and Dr. H. C. Mecklenburg, the District Superintendent, were the speakers for the occasion. They spoke of the sacred institution of the home and the sanctity of marriage, eloquently and at length.

At noon, the wedding party arrived. Gilbert was handsome in his rented suit and Hazel was a vision of loveliness in her white, fluffy gown with its gigantic train. The other members of the wedding party were appropriately attired. The ceremony, carried out with precision and dispatch, was flawless as any city wedding.

With Mrs. Ruth Lambdin at the reed organ, Margie Bowlin-Brown sang the old standards: "O Promise Me" and "I Love You Truly." Bob Green was the best man, and Mabel Henderson and Geraldine Petrey were bridesmaids. Dixie Rhinehart was ringbearer, and Anna Ruth Petrey, flower girl.

Parson Frakes read the ring ceremony, as *Life* photographers worked hard and fast to film every segment of the ceremony. Everything went off without a hitch, and, as the wedding march began, the happy couple left the church under the usual shower of rice, laughter, and good wishes.

One difference: the bride and groom didn't hurry off for their honeymoon after the cake-cutting. They stayed for the basket dinner, prepared for the wedding party and guests.

There were heaps of fried chicken, gallons of potato salad, drums of lemonade and ice tea, and loads of fresh vegetables and salads. It was truly a meal fit for a king; and *Life* made a photographic record for posterity.

When the article "Life at a Mountain Wedding" appeared in *Life,* Hazel and Gilbert received a lot of fan mail. It took them months to answer the mail that required an answer, and the article made for them a lot of friends. Of course, the coverage didn't hurt the Settlement either; for, although it was not the intention of the editors to promote the work there, the readers were able to read between the lines and to see the worthiness of the project.

Soon after Hazel and Gilbert were married, they left for Gilbert's farm in Indiana, where they live today. They have a family of five fine children. One son has returned, uninjured and highly decorated, from Vietnam, three have graduated from college; and the entire family is active in church and community affairs.

Little did Frakes think, when he took that first trek to Laurel Fork, that someday a major magazine like *Life* would make the journey over those rough, rocky roads, bringing thousands of dollars worth of equipment to photograph an event connected with his work. But by the grace of God it happened; and he was grateful and pleased —if not a little proud!

15.

THE WAY OF CAIN

The Parson had gone to his office after supper. His desk was stacked high with long-overdue letters. He had been so busy with routine Settlement business—repair of some plumbing, buying of supplies, and counseling with students—that his desk work had suffered from neglect.

As he picked up the first letter, Old Brutus, the Settlement collie, began to bark furiously. Frakes sighed as he looked at Mr. Kingon, his secretary. They both had hoped for a couple of uninterrupted hours to work. "Well, this will have to wait a minute," Frakes said, as he put the letter down. "Someone's coming up the path, that's for sure! I hope nothing else goes wrong today."

He had no more than said these words to Mr. Kingon, when there was a hard, loud knock at their door. Frakes silently wondered: Would it be about some woman in labor who needed to go to the hospital; or would it be news of some man injured in the mines? Bad news had been coming rather regularly these past few days, so he seemed to be bracing himself for this interruption.

As Frakes opened the door of his office, a young man pushed inside past him. Frakes noted that he looked very distraught and waited for him to speak.

"My brother's been shot, Preacher, and I think he's a-dyin'. You gotta' come right now. Maybe you can do something!"

Not stopping to question the boy, the Parson and Mr. Kingon grabbed their hats and followed him out the door.

As they hurried down the road in the Settlement truck, Frakes asked, "Do you know who shot him?"

The boy's lips tightened. It was an old code of the mountains: When someone is killed, keep your mouth shut. Even though it was his own brother who had been shot, he felt he dared not say a word about the man who had pulled the trigger.

The reasons for this are many. For one thing, if word got out that he was the one who had divulged the name of the culprit, he might be the victim of reprisal and revenge. Another reason was just plain fear. Those hills reeked with fear. Even though the Parson, with his healing balm of the Gospel, had been in those hills for ten years, the ghost of fear still lurked in those coves and valleys.

When two men met on the road, each man would plunge his right hand into his pocket, signalling to the other that he was armed. Even men who weren't armed would do this through force of habit, for it was standard procedure in the hills.

You see, not everyone in the valley had come under the influence of the church and the Christ the Parson exemplified. Many of them persisted in their ways, and the traditions that had been handed down to them from their fathers.

At the core of mountain thinking was the conviction that every man was an enemy until he had proved himself otherwise. Suspicion ran high, for it was bred into their very blood that even your nextdoor neighbor could be out to get you. Yet when these people learned to trust a person, they trusted him all the way. They also knew the meaning of loyal friendship and neighborliness but these had to be tried and tested and earned.

Frakes, however, through the church and the Settlement school, had brought a new dimension of friendship to the community. He was a friend to all the people. He had proved it, and the people trusted him. That's why the young man ran first to the Parson that night. He needed a friend, and he knew where one was. But even though he believed in Frakes and knew Frakes would help him, he was not about to give any details of the shooting to anyone.

With the young man sitting rigid and brokenhearted and noncommunicative in the corner of the front seat, the three men drove over the rough, stony road to the mouth of the creek. Because the road up Cornett's Branch was too rough and narrow for the truck, all three got out when the truck stopped and started to run up the little path beside the creek. They passed clusters of people who had heard of the shooting, had started out to learn more about it, but were too frightened to go further up the mountain.

The rumor was whispered about that the boy who had been shot was dead; and Frakes, as he rushed by, was informed of this. When the brother who had borne the news of the shooting to Frakes heard this, he became almost inconsolable. He grabbed the Parson by the shoulder, leaned on him, and sobbed unashamedly. Family ties are strong in the hills, and brotherly love runs deep.

Frakes put his arms around the boy and tried to comfort him, patting him kindly on the back.

"Why did he kill him?" the boy sobbed. "Oh, Parson, why did my brother have to be shot?"

"Come on, son, pull yourself together," Frakes said tenderly. "Let's go see what we can do. Maybe these people don't know."

The trio started again up the mountain. As they puffed their way to the top, a neighbor of Herb, the boy who had been shot, caught up with them, and filled the Parson in on the missing parts of the story.

It seems that Herb had gone to the aid of his sister Alice, whose husband Clive had come home drunk and started to beat her and their child. Clive then took his shotgun and shot the windows out of the house. This not being enough, he had shot at the floor, circling her feet. She, for fear of her life and the baby's, ran out the door and down the trail until she found a hiding place under a rock ledge near the creek bed.

Alice's parents and her brothers and sisters, who lived right across the ravine, heard the quarreling and then the shots. Without a moment's hesitation, they all started running toward Alice's cabin. They knew Clive was drunk, and they feared he had shot either Alice or the baby. They knew he was always irrational when he had been drinking.

As they ran breathlessly into the cabin of their daughter and sister, Clive was just standing there with the gun still smoking. Strangely enough, Clive did not menace them for their intrusion, as he usually would have done. Instead, upon seeing them arrive, he ran out the door and down the trail with his gun in his hands. He was still very angry.

As he went down the trail, he met Herb coming up to see what the shots were about. Herb and Alice had always been especially close, and Herb watched out for her like a mother hen, for he knew of Clive's meanness when he was drunk. It was probably this fact, along with the fact that Herb had quarreled with Clive the week before about his drunken abusiveness, that made Clive "see red." He let Herb pass, but decided right then that he was going to kill Herb, just as he had bragged he would to one of his friends that morning.

Herb was a good boy. He was the only one of the five sons in that family who didn't drink. He was a regular attendant at the Settlement Chapel, took part in the Saturday games, and was respected by everyone in the Laurel Fork area. His goodness, itself, was a constant rebuke to Clive.

Herb continued up the trail and joined his family. His father had arrived by this time and was in Alice's cabin. They discussed the situation for a few minutes, then decided to break up and all go look for Alice and the baby.

When Herb went down the trail to look for Alice, Clive was waiting for him behind a tree. Clive waited for Herb to get beyond the tree about ten paces. Then he took aim, pulled the trigger, shooting Herb through the back, and killing him instantly.

It was a scene so familiar to the mountains. There was no reason for Herb to die at gunpoint; there had only been a minor disagreement, in which he had made a point of Clive's being a poor husband. This was all it took, along with an overdose of alcohol.

Clive had threatened to his friend that he would murder Herb if he didn't stay out of his business. The seed was planted in his own heart. Then, finally, came the terrible, bloody act itself. It had been done scores, perhaps hundreds, of times in those mountains. Feelings ran very deep. Emotions were high and, too often, intelligence was low. The inevitable result was a shooting—too many of them like this one, from ambush. Though the work of the Settlement and the Parson's influence had curtailed the feuding and fighting tremendously, it would be overly-optimistic to assume that Laurel Fork had entered a millennium.

The Lord had led him to these people. The "happenings" involving guns and wounded or dead men were solemn reminders that the Parson's work was unfinished. One of his favorite scriptures was: "Where sin abounds, grace doth much more abound"—and it did!

Death always brought stark drama to the mountains. Most of the people lived in the shadow of it. Because of sickness, often due to malnutrition; the absence of physicians in the valley; or the old law of revenge and ruin—in one way or another, these people lived in the "valley of the shadow."

When death came, it threw out a cloak of despair and utter futility, especially for those families who had not opened their hearts to the hope of the Gospel.

Upon death's arrival, whether it came by the gun or by natural causes, the home of the deceased became a center of community interest and activity. As soon as the word got out that Herb had been shot and was dead, friends and neighbors, carrying their oil or carbide lanterns, lighted up the trails in the dark night. Muffled weeping and excited voices could be heard as the little groups made their way up the hill to the little, obscure cabin.

Inside, the people sat silently, awaiting the arrival of the body, which was being carried up the hill from the site of the shooting. Time was of the essence, for these mountain people had to be their own undertakers. Unless the body was "laid out" within an hour, rigor mortis would set in. Stout planks were used to carry the body, with the head being slightly elevated to prevent unnecessary discoloration.

When Herb's body arrived at the cabin, the men bathed it, dressed it in his Sunday best, and laid it again on the boards while the casket was being made.

The casket, made of plain boards, was similar to the rough boxes that caskets are crated in as they arrive at city mortuaries. When the casket had been finished by the mountain carpenters, the body was laid in it. It was then taken into the cabin to the accompaniment of the moans, screams, and laments of the family and friends, especially the women.

By this time, the mountain preachers arrived. Since the Johnsons were not members of the Parson's Settlement church, custom had it that a "mountain funeral" was most proper.

Now a mountain funeral is unlike anything else in the world. A death means lots of "preachin'." If three preachers come, there are three sermons. The occasion of death is used to remind the people of the brevity of life, according to the axiom that "life in the mountains is burdensome and brief." The preachers "line" out the hymns, and these are sung lustily by everyone present. One of the favorites is always:

> Will the circle be unbroken,
> By and by, by and by;
> In a better home awaiting,
> In the sky, in the sky.

Sometimes the services last all night, but, whether the service lasts all night or not, the neighbors and friends stay all night "asittin' with the body."

Herb's funeral followed the traditional pattern. As the mountain preacher, Brother Reeves, droned out the lines, the women took up the tune in shrill, broken voices, and were supported by the men's deep and firm bass. Then came the "exhortations," or sermons. Emotions ran high as the mountain preachers, punctuating their homilies with great gulping breaths, expounded in their sing-song tones. Women wept, and some of them shouted, as the preachers waxed eloquent about heaven and its beauties and joys.

The next day after dinner, Herb's body was taken to the cemetery, and they had another preaching service there. Herb's casket was left open to the sun and flies while the group sang hymns and the ministers gave their last exhortations. Then, as the end of the service came, Herb's mother, utterly broken, threw herself over the rough casket and sobbed out her deep grief and loss. He was her youngest and finest, the one who always helped her in times of need or stress; the one the whole family depended on for sanity and guidance. How could she give him up? The other members of the family had to literally lift her away from her dear son's casket.

As the people filed down the slope from the mountain graveyard, Frakes stood outside the group with an aching heart. He, along with many of the people from the Settlement, had come to pay their "respects" to Herb. Herb had been one of their finest young men, and the settlement would feel his loss. Frakes, as he watched the people leave, vowed again that he would work harder than ever to stamp out senseless killings like Herb's, and all the other evils and inequities of Laurel Fork.

The judge in Pineville gave Clive sixteen years for shooting Herb; but somehow Clive didn't quite get the message that he was being punished. He wrote a letter to one of his brothers from state prison:

You wouldn't believe how fine things are here at the prison. They feed you three good meals every day, and we have a warm room to sleep in at night. The work ain't bad, and we'uns gets a lot o' time to play cards, see movies, and stuff like that. I never knew prison life could be so fine.

Poor Herb was dead, and Clive had just begun to live. Well, maybe they were both better off. For Herb had said after the revival in the Settlement Chapel during the summer: "After Mr. Kingon's talk about Christ dying for my sin, I felt a change come over me, and I haven't been the same person since."

It was statements like this, in this never-never land of superstition, hate, and lawlessness, that convinced the Parson that his life was being used for the glory of God. Hundreds in the valley could match Herb's testimony.

16.

AND KNOWLEDGE SHALL BE INCREASED

One hundred seventy-one years ago Abraham Lincoln was born in Rolling Fork, Larue County, Kentucky. The desire for wisdom, knowledge, and understanding was always present in the son of Tom Lincoln. He became a man of integrity and insight not in spite of, but because of his surroundings. He grasped even the slightest wisp of knowledge and stored it away in his great mind and heart. Like Moses, who was also an emancipator, he used and utilized what he had at hand. This Lincoln-like quality of doing the best with what one has to work with is a characteristic of many of the people of Appalachia. All their lives they have to "make do" with inadequate tools and facilities. They are by nature great innovators. Even the children of Laurel Fork have inherited this admirable quality.

The fame of the Settlement had spread far and wide by 1938, principally through the work of the Parson, who had the knack of letting people know what God was doing in Laurel Fork. Partin Hall, with its tremendous opportunities and challenges, was soon bursting at the seams.

When funds for the school got low, the Parson hitched up his mule, drove through the almost impassable mud to Chenoa, hopped a freight train, picked up his car in Pineville, and drove far and wide to "hawk" his wares among the benevolent folk of Methodism. Usually he brought home the "bacon."

The situation in the valley was encouraging. Moonshining was now becoming little more than a memory.

Law and order were at an all-time high. Prize poultry was being raised, and profitable crops were being harvested on the hitherto fallow and unproductive ground. Church attendance was up, and the fall revival was the greatest in the history of the work, with scores baptized.

For five years Partin Hall served the school needs of the Settlement. The building was heated by two hot-air furnaces, which were inadequate and needed repair. A new steam heating plant would cost $2,100 and, with the mounting expense of housing children in the dormitory and the increased school attendance, it was out of the question.

During an extreme cold spell in the winter of 1939, one of the boys went to stoke the fire and discovered that the basement was full of smoke and flames. He yelled for help, and forty men, who were working nearby on a road, rushed to the scene to extinguish the fire. The smoke was so bad they could not gain entrance to the basement. They cut a hole in the first floor, hoping to let the smoke escape; but when they did, the hole created a draft, and the flames leaped up through the chapel to the third story dormitory. Nothing could be done to save the building.

Frakes and his wife had been in Pineville. When he and Mrs. Frakes returned to the Settlement, all that was left of their beloved Partin Hall were charred walls and glowing embers. It had been the center of all Settlement activity—home, school, and church—for five years.

The children stood around the rubble and wept openly. Strong, rough mountaineers, after losing their fight to save the building, stood helplessly on the sidelines as the flames, helped by a strong wind, leveled the building they had worked so hard to build. With tears trickling down their tough, brawny faces, at least fifty men stood in mute silence and watched the very heart of their work burn to the ground.

Partin Hall was gone; but the spirit that built it lived on. Sixteen boys, who had been living on the third floor of Partin Hall, gathered around the charred remains of their home. Their faces wore a mask as though in the presence of death; they were pensive and quiet, as they faced the reality of their situation. Their circumstances looked mighty bleak. In one day, it appeared, they had lost not only their chance for an education, but also their security. One of the boys told the Parson almost hysterically, "We've lost our clothes, our books, and everything we have. None of us here has a thing left but what we have on."

Frakes tried to console the boys, but, at the moment, he too was at a loss to know what to do. Then the mountain people began to arrive with their offers of hospitality. Many of them volunteered to take the children who had lived in the dormitory to their homes until some improvised quarters could be arranged for them. Slowly things began to look brighter.

The day after the fire, twelve men of the community arrived to help build a temporary school. The old sawmill was fired up again. Some of the men sawed lumber, others began to make partitions in the tabernacle, where the community activities took place; and the unfinished new church was utilized, with makeshift partitions dividing the area into small rooms. The men set to work to make desks, benches, and tables. Long after dark, the sounds of hammers and saws were heard. Stoves were moved in for heating, and, after only three days without classes, the old school bell rang again. It was all a marvelous miracle. The improvised school, with stovepipes jutting out of the windows and through the roof was no Partin Hall; but the children were warm and happy. At least, they had the reassurance that someone cared for them.

More than sixty men signed a paper pledging to give from five-to-ten days' free time to rebuild Partin Hall. They had little money to give, so they offered what they had—strong hands, considerable skills, and willing hearts.

Christian sympathy, understanding, and generosity

from throughout the Cumberland range flowed into Laurel Fork. Gifts came from the most unexpected sources. The Coal Miner's Union at Pruden, Tennessee, seven miles across the mountain, sent word for Frakes to come to the Union Hall to receive a contribution from the mine workers. The coal company at Pruden sent word that they would match the amount that the miners gave. Friends up in the blue grass section of Kentucky offered to buy the heating plant for the new building. A gift of $500 was also received to equip the home economics and manual training departments. "The Lord giveth and the Lord taketh away." It appeared that the Lord was going to give much more than had been taken away.

In the Spring, when the thaws began and the weather was moderating, the sounds of hammers and saws filled Laurel Fork valley. The people, like those in Nehemiah's day, "had a mind to work." From Pineville and Middlesboro came carpenters with willing hands and needed tools. From Indiana to the north, and Virginia to the east, tradesmen came to offer a day, a week, or even a month of free labor. But most of the construction force came from Laurel Fork, where many of the workers, with strong backs and special skills, contributed to the emergence of a Parson's dream and their own fondest hopes.

On Sunday, July 21, 1940, the building was dedicated. Songs of victory rang throughout the chapel as hundreds thanked God for the miracle they had seen emerge—the new Partin Hall. High on the hill where the first Partin Hall had stood, the new building towered, a sentinel of faith and vision, a tribute to a living God and a living Gospel, which made it all possible.

Governor Sampson, who had himself been born in a log cabin in the mountains of Kentucky, said of the new school:

> No one can calculate the great good that this and other similar schools in Eastern Kentucky will do. Not only academic subjects are taught, but students are taught how to live together happily. They are taught how to serve others,

how to plant orchards, how to plant and harvest crops, how to do dairying, how to plan homes and rear children, how to raise poultry, and other useful occupations. Throughout Laurel Fork valley, the crude bare cabins are being converted into more comfortable and better furnished homes. There is peace and contentment everywhere. The strong, agile, healthy, eager boys and girls of this rugged country, who display their brilliancy of mind and aptitude by conforming to new conditions and mastering the most difficult subjects, constitute one of the state's most valuable assets and priceless potentialities. Kentucky is proud of the accomplishment of these schools in the few brief years of their existence. Let not the door of opportunity be closed against them, or against the youth of the Appalachian highlands which they serve.

School opened in the new Partin Hall with an overwhelming increase in attendance. The faith that it took to bring the new building to reality seemed to be reflected in a new interest in education and in all the projects of the Settlement. New teachers had to be added to the staff: a nurse, an accredited principal, and all the others essential to a modern institution of learning.

Opening day of the new school was exciting for the children. The Rev. W. E. Cissna, the new principal, tells us in his own words: "Monday morning. School begins today. The first bell in the new dormitory rang at 5 A.M., and breakfast was served at 5:30. As I entered the porch leading to the dorm, I met a boy, who appeared to be about nine years old. His feet were muddy, as it had rained very hard during the night. I asked why he had come so early, and he said that he had to walk four miles to school and he didn't want to be late.

"School began at eight o'clock. By 7 A.M., crowds of boys and girls were happily plodding along through the rain and mud on their way to the big new school on the hill.

"I marvelled at how quiet and reverent the pupils became as they entered the school. From my office, I could not help but notice that the loud and boisterous spirit usually found in school halls was missing. I could hardly believe, as the last school bell was rung, that 172 boys and girls had gathered in their respective homerooms and were ready for school to begin.

"After the pupils were enrolled, then came the chapel service with the joyful singing, the talks, and the prayers. Then the county health nurse started her examinations, bringing to light many who were underweight, had bad teeth and poor eyesight.

" 'That boy,' said a teacher to me, pointing to a slim undernourished little fellow, 'walked six and one-half miles to school, and it's the first time he has ever attended a school anywhere.' He was eleven years old. The average distance walked by the children was over two miles, and some walked as much as seven or eight miles ungrudgingly.

"No wonder they come to Partin Hall! The new educational, spiritual, and social center of the Settlement. Here they find college-trained teachers, a large library of good reading books, modern seats and desks, plenty of pencils, tables, pens, and ink, wall maps, globes, blackboards, up-to-date school books, and well-lighted, clean rooms in which to study and recite. Not to mention the teachers, who cared enough for them to forego the luxuries of a more modern community just to give the mountain children a chance for a good education."

By this, the tenth year of the Settlement's growth, the little village of Henderson Settlement boasted of much more than a new school. There were other buildings cropping up on the land so lovingly given by Bill Henderson, Scott Partin, and other people of the community. There was an office, a carpenter's shop, a blacksmith shop, barns for the sturdy mules and horses, a weaving building, where an expert weaver taught the women to weave, and where the woven articles would be offered for sale. There was also the "cozy cottage," where the women teachers lived. It was an old building, but it had been transformed by loving hands into a thing of beauty. The Settlement has its own water system, its own waterworks, and its own small telephone system, with phones connected to each building. But the Settlement's principal wealth is people; for these mountain people, all who had a part in its development, have willingly sacrificed and worked.

The Bell County Board of Education had decided to consolidate the three outlying mountain districts, which channeled 350 students into the new Partin Hall. A new school bus was put in operation to transport children who lived too far away to walk. In the $30,000 building, with ten large classrooms, a manual training shop, a home economics kitchen, and some offices, the teachers could do a much more effective job. It was as fine a school building as any in the county, and better than most; and most of the funds came from loving hearts and willing hands, with little cost to the federal and county agencies.

On opening day, as the Parson stood adjacent to the school watching the children file out on their way home to their mountain cabins, their books under their arms, laughing or smiling happily, he whispered to an aid, "Except the Lord build the house, they labor in vain that build it." The Lord had built this house, and his work was not in vain. Others filed bigger income taxes than Parson Frakes, and many had more stocks and bonds, but few had the inner satisfaction or the blessing that he had in seeing his valley—formerly so fraught with violence and illegal activities—now become a little heaven on earth. He was humbly grateful and satisfied with his lot in life.

17.

A GIRL'S DREAM COME TRUE

Dovey Rogers, a thirteen-year-old child of the mountains, sloshed through the red mud on the way home from the clapboard cabin they called a school. The events of the day, which were typical of all days in that mountain school, raced through her mind. She had worked every problem in the tattered arithmetic book four times or more, and she knew she couldn't make any further progress because there were no new books available. Besides this, the teacher couldn't work any harder problems, for this is as far as his education had taken him.

"What can I do," Dovey asked herself out loud, "to get a proper education? I might as well get married like the rest of the girls in our valley," she mused, "and start raisin' children. There's no need for me to go back to school."

That night, after a typical mountain supper of fatback and fried potatoes, Dovey was more quiet than usual. Her mother watched her silently for a time, wondering what was bothering her child.

Finally the mother said, "You got sumthin' on yer mind, Dovey. What is it?"

"Nothin', Mom. I was jest a-thinkin'."

"A-thinkin' what?" the mother prodded.

"I was a-thinkin' thet it ain't doin' me no good to walk them three miles through the mud to school when I ain't larnin' nothin' new or worthwhile."

"Why, Dovey! You've always sed you wanted to git an edication, and be different from the other young'uns in these h'yar hills."

A GIRL'S DREAM COME TRUE

"Yeh, Mom, I know," Dovey agreed, "but I'll never git it in that thar school I'm a-goin' to. My teacher's never bin eny further in school than I've gone. I jest keep a-doin' the same work over and over."

Dovey's mother knew she was right, for she'd been concerned about this for some time. So much so that she'd been asking lots of questions every time she saw a stranger in the valley. Why, just today, a strange man had ridden by and had come back for a drink of water. She wondered if she dare tell Dovey what he'd told her about a school.

"Dovey," the mother said almost apprehensively, "a man was by h'yar today en' sed he'd heerd of a school over in Kentucky where they have new books, edicated teachers, en' a place whar the kids kin stay and work their way through school. He sed it was called, let's see, . . . I think he sed it sumthin' like 'Henderson Settlement.' Now, I don't know if'n he was right, but that's whut he sed!"

Dovey's despair left her immediately, for here was hope. "Oh, Mom," she said excitedly, "do you s'pose he was? I sure would like to go on and git an edication. He said hit's jest over the ridge yonder."

The two were quiet for a moment as they considered the possibilities. It wasn't easy for mountain people to make drastic changes or decisions. Suddenly, Dovey jumped up from her chair and ran to throw her arms around her mother. She had a wonderful idea, and she needed her mother's support. "Mom," she said, hugging her mother, "you know whut? Tomorrow's Saturday. Why don't you en' me make our way over to that Henderson place and see whut it is. We could git up real early and do it, I know we could! If'n I could go on to school I'd be the happiest girl in these hyar mountains."

According to her mother's calculations, Henderson Settlement must be at least ten miles over the mountains. That was a long way for two women to go alone. She didn't even like to think about it; but then . . . she remembered this might be Dovey's only chance. "We'll hev to think about it, Dovey," she said. "We'uns cain't jump up and do somethin' foolish."

That night Dovey could hardly sleep. Some children are born with a greater awareness of their destiny than others, and Dovey was one of these. She had always felt, down in her heart, that somehow, someway, she could be used to help the children of her section to learn and to improve their way of living. She didn't know quite how; but she was sure that someday it would all happen. That Henderson place—whatever it was—was her first "open door." If it taught beyond the fourth grade, she wanted to go. It could be the first step to the fulfillment of the dream she'd had as long as she could remember. Yes, if tomorrow was a nice day, she'd beg her mother to help her find it. She knew it wouldn't be easy; but she must do it. Yes, she must!

The sun was shining brightly when Dovey got up the next morning, and the warm April breezes were coaxing the frost out of the winter ground. She could smell the fatback frying in the next room of their little cabin. Her mind, still fuzzy from sleep, kept trying to remind her of something she was going to do today. Then, there it was! That wonderful Henderson place; . . . she must go today.

She ran in to her mother who was now frying an egg, and started her plea, "Mom, it's a wonderful day! The sun is out, so it won't be so cold. Couldn't we please go today?"

"But, Dovey, I figure hit's at least nine or ten miles," her mother reminded her, "and it won't be easy to find."

"Oh, Mom, we can find it, I jist know we can," Dovey persisted. "Let's hurry and eat our breakfast and pack a little lunch, and at least try! Please, Mom, I want to so much, en' we kin be home afore dark."

Dovey's widowed mother couldn't resist her excitement and pleading; so within an hour they were on their way.

The man had told Dovey's mother that Laurel Fork was "just over the ridge yonder." With faith in those instructions, they started in that direction. They walked up the creek bank, over the steep hills covered with undergrowth, and across the mountain pass; but still they didn't see any valley. They trudged on along a mountain trail, climbed fences, and crossed a broad creek several times. They cut across fields with weeds as tall as they were; and when the sun was high in the sky, they stopped by a cool stream to eat their hurriedly packed lunch. Feeling refreshed, they continued their search, as they walked on toward the high ridge, which was much closer now. As they climbed up the rock-jutted slope, they stepped carefully, watching for snakes. They were too excited now to think of how tired they were; they just knew they must go on until they found what they were looking for.

Finally, they reached the summit of the mountain; and Dovey's eyes widened with joy, as she and her mother looked down on a valley that widened into a broad vista.

"That's it, Mom," Dovey exclaimed, as she jumped up and down in her excitement. "It has to be!"

Nestled below them in the green valley was an orderly world such as Dovey had never dreamed of. Clustered together like a citadel were the gleaming white school building, a sturdy modern dormitory, the painted barns and sheds, and all kinds of beautiful modern-looking buildings, cleaner and more attractive than any the two had ever seen.

"Oh, Mom, isn't it like another world?" Dovey asked as she surveyed the sight. "Could it be that I might be living there one day?"

The mother squeezed her daughter's hand. So much was involved in her bringing Dovey to this place. She could barely bring herself to think of separation from Dovey; but she must not think of herself now. Bravely she smiled at Dovey and said, "Let's go see."

Clutching each other's hands, they walked without speaking down to the stately buildings. As they arrived, some children ran out to greet them and offered them a cool drink of water. It was obvious the two had come a long way. Their clothes had been torn some by the briers along the way, and their faces were red from their hurried climb up the ridge; but the two had more important things to think of.

The mother spoke to the children timidly, "Could you please take us to the one in charge?"

One of the girls of the group took over, saying kindly, "Oh, yes. He's right over there in his office. I'll take you. Just follow me."

Frakes was busy with his usual letter writing; but he welcomed Dovey and her mother warmly and invited them into his office. He could tell they were here "with purpose."

Dovey had told her mother that she wanted to make her own appeal to whoever was in charge. Even as young as she was, she knew she was better qualified than her mother; for she had already had much more education.

Dovey immediately started to tell Frakes about her dream of a better education, and about the limitations of the little school near her home. She told him of the man her mother had talked with the day before, of their long search today, and of how she had prayed it wasn't a false story they'd been told.

Frakes listened intently as the little girl poured out her heart. He was impressed by her eagerness and deep desire. She was a "special" one, all right! Finally, he broke into her anxious selling job with, "Dovey, do you realize that if you were to come here to school, you would have to stay here for five or six years? And that you'd be separated from your mother for a very long time?"

Dovey shook her head up and down happily.

"Do you know," Frakes continued, "that you'd have to work after school during the winter, and all summer long to pay for your room and board?"

Seeing she was still most agreeable to this arrangement, he went on, "Dovey, some of the work is hard. There is canning to do in the summer, and lots of cleaning. Sometimes our girls even have to work in the garden."

He noticed that Dovey was pondering his questions,

and that all seemed acceptable, but he went on, just to be sure. "There's lots of washing and ironing to do all winter long, after school; and the girls take turns doing that, or doing the cooking or the cleaning. Would you be willing to give up much of your free time for an education, Dovey?"

Dovey knew it was a big order. Her life had been carefree in the little cabin with her mother. She had enjoyed the leisurely life she'd had. Nothing had ever been hard for her, and this, she realized, would be a whole new life. She'd have to leave her childhood behind if she wanted an education. After reviewing Frakes's penetrating questions completely, she looked up at Frakes, took a deep breath, and said, "Yes, Mr. Frakes, in some ways, it will be very hard; but I understand whut you've bin saying, en' I'm willing to do whut you say."

Tears stood at the rim of Dovey's eyes as she looked to her widowed mother for confirmation. Hard as it was for Dovey's mother to give it, she did, and Dovey saw that she had it.

Frakes saw the determined set of Dovey's jaw as she spoke to him, and he felt satisfied that this girl should be admitted to his school. You see, he had many applicants, and he had to make sure he made the right selections. He had learned something else; children rise to a tough challenge, and he felt Dovey would be no exception.

As the interview was coming to a close, the Parson decided he might as well give Dovey the full treatment while she was in an agreeable mood. During their talk he had noticed that Dovey was wallowing something around in her mouth, something so large that her cheek protruded. Wise to mountain children's habits, he knew there was no mistake as to what it was. So he said, "Dovey, there's something else I must say to you. You know, if you come to our dormitory to live, you'll have to give up that chewing tobacco."

The girl was a bit startled, because it was the first time anyone had ever challenged her habit. She lowered her head and said, a little ashamedly, "I'll give it a try, sir."

On the way back home, her heart was light and gay. Mr. Frakes had told her she could come and live in the dormitory and attend the Settlement school. She and her mother talked of nothing else all the way home. Together, they dreamed of the day when she would have her diploma from high school, and of all the things she might do. The two had walked eighteen miles that day, over mountains, down slopes, through fields of briars and weeds, and across creeks; but it was worth it all, they both agreed. Dovey was going to a real school! The future held promise, promise of a dream come true!

The very next week Dovey left her mother and the little mountain cabin for the new life at the Settlement. It was a sad farewell for the two. Both realized it was the end of an era for both of them. With all her earthly belongings in a package under her arm, Dovey started out alone, waving to her mother until she was completely out of sight.

Like Abraham, she was going out, not knowing where she was going, but confident that she was going in the right direction. She walked the nine miles all alone, retracing the steps she had made with her mother the week before.

Arriving at the Settlement in the early evening, she was shown to the room that she would share with some other girls. She unpacked and "settled in." Immediately, she fit into the life there beautifully, just as though she were tailor-made for it.

After a week on the campus, she met the Parson in front of the dormitory and greeted him with, "Mr. Frakes, I'm all done with my tobaccer. I ain't had a chaw in four days!"

Dovey was an excellent student with sterling character. In five years she completed her elementary schooling and graduated from high school with honors. She became a member of the Sunbonnet Girls' quartette and traveled with the Parson to many corners of the Methodist world, telling the people of many other girls like herself, tucked away in the Tennessee and Kentucky mountains, who had absolutely no chance for an education unless someone helped and cared.

One day, in an interview with Dovey, Mr. Frakes asked her, "Dovey, you've graduated from high school now and completed this phase of your progress. What do you plan to do now?"

Without a moment's hesitation she answered, "I'd like most of all to get some nurse's training. My people need a registered nurse. I think I'd like to become one and come back here and help my people."

Arrangements were made for Dovey to enter the Deaconess Hospital in Louisville, Kentucky. Because of her high scholastic record, she was granted a scholarship. In three years, Dovey completed the nurse's training and became an RN.

Upon her graduation the superintendent of the hospital said to Mr. Frakes, "Do you have any more girls in those mountains like Dovey? If you do, send them to us. We could use fifteen like her."

Dovey didn't return to the mountains right away, but she served humanity just the same. Immediately upon graduating, Dovey became employed by the Veterans Hospital in Louisville; and, later, was sent to the "Atomic City," Oak Ridge, Tennessee, to help reorganize the health unit there as that city was transferred from military to civilian status.

During her tenure at the Hospital in Louisville, she met a young man who had grown up in her own mountains. They fell in love and were married. It seemed that Dovey's dream had been detoured a bit; but, not for long.

Shortly after her marriage, a call came for Dovey to go back to her Tennessee mountains to work for the Rural Health Service. Three nurses had attempted to qualify for the job but had failed; and this opened the way for Dovey. Happily, she accepted the call she had been waiting for through the years. She went to the little isolated county, hidden back in the hills of Tennessee, where she is serving her people today. Dovey's dream had come true.

It had been a long journey from that first walk over the mountain with her mother. There had been the surrendering of her tobacco, along with the other disciplines of learning and living; the circuitous twists of destiny; the marrying of a boy from her own country; and finally, her assignment to serve her own people, whom she loved, and the fulfillment of her life's ambition and dream. But, by the help of the good Lord and Parson Frakes, she made it!

18.

BLACK FRIDAY

When I accepted the invitation to be pastor, coach, medical officer, and bandmaster of the high school at the Settlement, Betty my wife and I were excited about the prospects and challenges of Laurel Fork. We knew we were inheriting many advantages that the Parson had obtained by hard work and sacrifice. We knew, also, that we had not come to the Settlement for "just another job." As a matter of fact, we were taking a big cut in our income—and this with three young children to support. But we were convinced this was the job the Lord wanted us to do, so nothing could stop us. Although the large and flourishing church we were serving in Indiana was mission-minded, most of the people couldn't understand why we would go to such an isolated corner of the world. "Why," they argued, "should a young couple work for one hundred dollars a month, when they could get three or four times that amount?"

Money itself had never been the chief measuring stick for Betty and me when it came to making a decision about where we should serve in the Lord's kingdom. So we came to the Settlement with happy hearts, really excited about the prospect of seeing the work grow into even greater proportions than ever. We knew the Lord had a way of compensating people who served him faithfully, and we were convinced that no one could beat the Lord in a game of "giveaway." We felt that relying on this was the only way to live. We had known and pitied preachers whose first question was always: "How much are you getting?" We had found the only satisfying question for a Christian worker was: "How much are you giving?"

We moved into the new parsonage (that was the first bonus) next to Kynett Chapel, which was also new, with our hearts beating expectantly, and with stars in our eyes. It was a quiet, serene location, and the surrounding country was beautiful. The people were lovable, friendly, and responsive. The staff at the Settlement was the greatest; and Frakes himself was like a great big lovable Kentucky mountain bear. It was all too wonderful; we had never been happier.

One of the first things I did was to organize a Men's Brotherhood. Years before, they had had a Community Welfare League, a group of men who believed in "law, order, and decency," but this organization hadn't met for a long time. We felt that, just as the women had their fellowship, the children got together at school, the men needed to get together too. They needed to talk over the problems of the community, and to exercise old-fashioned neighborliness. The men responded overwhelmingly to the idea.

The Brotherhood met once a month. We promised the men a "good feed"—which in the squirrel season was always Brunswick stew. The men loved it. What could be better for a mountain man than squirrel meat mixed with fresh vegetables, corn, carrots, peas, and cabbage out of the Settlement garden! When you put that down with lots of coffee, iced tea, or milk, and, of course, thick slices of homemade bread, and country butter, you've won the heart of a mountain man. As the mountain women always say, "A man's heart is close to his stomach."

I looked forward to these Brotherhood meetings. They were the high spots of the monthly activities and, to my way of thinking, the most rewarding.

Just to watch the men gather in the churchyard wearing their freshly laundered blue jeans, khaki shirts, and square-toed brogan shoes or high leather boots—freshly shined, if you please—was a pleasure.

On a certain warm, spring Friday evening toward the last of May, we had more men than usual. Evidently, the east wind had carried the aroma of that delicious Brunswick stew clear through Laurel Fork valley, and the men were automatically drawn to that churchyard and the old tabernacle, where we held our dinner meetings. By 5:30 P.M., there were twenty-five or thirty men present, squatting on their haunches in a circle, in their characteristic manner. This was the mountain way of relaxing, practiced throughout those hills.

The first to arrive was Sherd Partin, our deputy sheriff, and the only law officer in Laurel Fork. Sherd was one of the finest men in the community; he was a faithful attendant at church, and a good family man. He was the father of Elmer Partin, the farm manager and Sunday school superintendent. Sherd had made his decision for Christ in a revival we had conducted a year ago, and has been one of the most dedicated Christians we have ever known.

Sherd didn't throw his weight around. He was a good law officer, but he wasn't aggressive. (It didn't pay to be in those hills.) But when a man got out of line, and it was obvious to all observers that he was breaking the law, Sherd went into action quickly and decisively.

Practically all the Partin men had arrived, and there were plenty of them. There were Scott, Ernest, Wade, Tilden, Ed, Evan, and Elmer—and many more. The Partins comprised about 80 percent of the population of Laurel Fork, and many a girl named "Partin," married a distant cousin and never even changed her name. My wife and I used to jokingly say, if you don't know a person's name, you'll probably be safe to call him "Partin."

The men were getting a bit restless and hungry; my wife was a little late in calling "come and get it!"

One man got up and began to stretch. He looked down

the road and said, "Well, I swanee, if'n that don't look like Hilliard and Robert a-comin' to our meetin'!"

"Naw, those two ain't a-comin' to our meetin', I'll guarantee ya' that," Wade Partin said. "They got interests besides a Brutherhood meetin'!"

Robert and Hilliard had been in our revival a year ago, had come right to the point of decision, but had stubbornly refused to make a profession of their faith in Christ. Oddly, from that day on, they had gone down, both in their own eyes, and in the estimation of others. Rumor had it that they had a still just beyond the Settlement property. They boasted openly that they had stolen some corn from the Settlement farm to "run off their first batch of whiskey."

When Wade mentioned their other "interests," most of the men got up to see the two men coming slowly and deliberately up the road. When the two reached the churchyard fence, to everyone's surprise, they turned, jumped over the fence, ignoring the steps built over it, and walked toward the group without saying a word. To mountain men, silence was eloquent; the quieter a conversation, the more meaningful it became to them. When Robert and Hilliard jumped over that fence and joined the group, everyone sensed something was wrong. You could feel the tension in the air, but still no one said a word.

Suddenly Hilliard said angrily, "What the hell's goin' on around here? You all a-goin' to have a lynchin' 'er somethun?"

Sherd slowly walked over to the two men, and said in a low voice, "You fellows behave, 'er I'll have to take you to town."

Robert replied belligerently, "The next time I go to town, I'm a-goin' *for* somethun!"

Since he was daring Sherd, there was nothing left for him to do. He had to make an arrest, charging "disturbing the peace." He said, "You fellows stay right where you are. You are under arrest, and, after this meetin's over, I'm a-takin' you into Pineville."

The air was tense. Sherd scowled at the men as they seemed to enjoy some private joke, which apparently was about Sherd. They appeared to be waiting for a secret cue to openly defy Sherd. "Don't you move, either of you," Sherd commanded. "Do you hear me?"

The Brotherhood men returned to their haunch-sitting positions so as to not get involved. They were trying to be nonchalant about this whole affair. They thought by doing so, they might end it.

Suddenly Sherd leaped toward Hilliard, grabbed him around the waist, and said, "Give me that gun!"

Sherd's sharp, trained eyes had seen the slender, undernourished-looking Hilliard reach into the deep right-hand pocket of his blue overalls, in which he kept his .38 pistol. It was common knowledge that Hilliard had boasted often that someday he was going to kill that d____ deputy, and nobody could stop him.

Sherd wrestled Hilliard down the slope into the circle of squatting men. Hilliard now had his .38 in his right hand, and Sherd, sensing his predicament, held Hilliard with his strong left hand as he worked his own pistol out of the holster.

Now, each had his pistol at the ready. Each was trying to maneuver the other into a position where he could get a shot at his opponent with his gun.

It was obvious that Sherd's was a defensive action; but it was equally obvious that Hilliard intended to "do Sherd in," if at all possible.

Later, it was learned that the assailant had just acquired four cartridges for his .38, and had told several of his cohorts that at least one of those shells was for Sherd. "I'm a-goin' to put it right into his heart," he had bragged.

The whole thing happened so fast that I was stunned, as were all the other men squatting around. They hadn't even time to get up off their haunches.

It all seemed like a nightmare. It just could not possibly be happening! But it was, and it looked like a battle to the death.

Unarmed, and believing Sherd could handle almost any situation, all of us there were almost paralyzed when we realized that Hilliard had the upper hand. There seemed to be nothing we could do to ameliorate the predicament Sherd was in.

Hilliard had the longer arms of the two, and was trying hard to get his gun around Sherd's stout body so he could shoot him in the back. Suddenly, there was a pistol report! Hilliard's gun had gone off, but he missed Sherd, and the slug went whizzing off through the tops of the trees. Then it fired again, as the determined assailant tried to kill Sherd on the spot.

At this point, Sherd stumbled over a large rock, Hilliard realized his advantage and threw him backward, and Sherd's pistol dropped to the ground with a fateful thud.

Now our law officer was without a gun; and a violent, irrational man had a loaded pistol—and a burning desire to finish the job he'd begun.

Awakened fully now to the tragic situation, I looked for a chance to enter the fray. But the two men were moving swiftly, and the gun seemed to be everywhere.

I stood there with the other men in helpless frozen fury. My heart was beating wildly, and I have never experienced a greater feeling of utter helplessness.

Finally, Hilliard, with his long right arm, maneuvered his gun viciously into the center of Sherd's back. He fired two shots, and Sherd fell limp to the ground.

Without a moment's hesitation Hilliard and Robert, their mission completed, ran off through the dense woods on the other side of the old Tabernacle. Hilliard's pistol was still smoking as he ran.

Some of the men had not risen from their squatting position during the fight. But when they saw the drama coming to its closing stages, like men leaving a theater after the picture has ended, they got up and began to move around.

BLACK FRIDAY

As Hilliard took long, fast strides up the gentle slope where he would be safe, it suddenly dawned on me that he had killed a man, and he was getting away. I could not believe that no one was pursuing him.

My mind was in a muddle. I was angry, confused, almost beside myself, but I knew what I had to do! I had to catch that man.

I took off after him! I ran as fast as I could toward the woods where Hilliard had disappeared. It seemed now that I possessed almost supernatural power. I could not undo the killing, but it still wasn't too late to keep the killer from going free.

I ran as I had never run before. I'm sure I beat my high school time of 10.5 for 100 yards. When I came to a turn in the trail, I saw Hilliard ahead and knew I was gaining on him. He was still carrying the pistol in his hand. I didn't know whether he had any more cartridges or not; and at this stage I didn't care.

Within seconds I drew up alongside him. He didn't even attempt to draw his gun as I reached out and grabbed his arm. His gun fell to the ground. Then, exerting all the strength I could muster, I grasped his other arm, tightened my grip, and forced him to his knees.

He looked up at me with wild, trapped eyes, and pleaded, "Preacher, let go of me. Oh my God, . . . I say, let go of me. They'll kill me."

"You killed Sherd," I accused him, gasping for breath.

"Oh Lordy, oh Lordy! Let go of me, Preacher," he prayed and begged at the same time.

I tightened my hold on him. His pleas had no effect on me, for he had killed my friend. He was a murderer without a cause, and I was determined he would pay for his crime.

As I held on to him firmly, giving him no chance to escape, I heard someone approaching through the light brush. The saplings parted, and I saw it was Elmer, Sherd's twenty-five-year-old son.

Elmer was late in coming to the Brotherhood meeting, so he had missed the murderous scene. He had apparently arrived just after I had taken off to catch Hilliard.

"Did he shoot my pappy?" he demanded.

"Yes, he did, Elmer, and I think Sherd is dying."

"I just saw him," Elmer said angrily, "and I know he is. Preacher, give him to me."

"No, Elmer," I tried to reason, "enough harm's been done. He'll not hurt anyone now. We'll take him to Pineville."

Elmer's face was white with rage. "Preacher, I said give him to me!"

I tried to cover Hilliard with my body to protect him; but Elmer was beside himself. He brusquely pulled me aside, as he faced Hilliard and said, "You killed my pappy!"

I stood back. My heart was beating madly as I realized another crisis had arisen. My brain was numb from the unreal events of the last few minutes.

Elmer took Hilliard's slender arms and put his hands together and clasped them tightly with his strong left hand. He reached inside his coat pocket with his free right hand.

I stood stunned, thinking he was reaching for a gun. But instead of a gun Elmer pulled a blackjack out of his pocket. He swung the menacing weapon and hit Hilliard on the top of the head, again and again. The blood began to spurt from Hilliard's head, as he prayed for his very life. "Don't kill me! Don't kill me!" he cried, as the blood flowed down over his head.

It was obvious that Elmer in his boundless rage had made himself for the moment both judge and jury. He was going to see to it that Hilliard got his due.

Finally, exhausted from his bludgeoning retribution, he stopped.

I lifted Hilliard up by the arms and stood him on his feet. He stumbled along after me, with Elmer behind him. We led him back to the group of men. Some had gained presence of mind enough to try to help Sherd, and my wife had put a pillow under his head. But it was apparent that Sherd had been mortally wounded.

Thinking the horrible fracas was surely over, I had begun to breathe almost normally again, when I heard a man running toward the group.

It was Tilden Partin, Sherd's brother. Tilden, although friendly to the Settlement, had never embraced Christianity, and had killed three men. He had heard the shooting and the shouting and had run the mile and a half from his house to see what was happening.

When he arrived, he surveyed the situation instantly. He saw his brother's face pale with death. He saw Sherd's pistol, dropped during the scuffle with Hilliard, lying on the ground by Sherd's body. Then he saw Elmer and me, with Hilliard in tow.

He asked the group in general, "Wait! Did that _____ _____ _____ shoot my brother?"

One man answered for the group, fearfully, "Yes, . . . he did, Tilden."

Tilden's face flushed red with rage. He picked up Sherd's pistol, checked it for ammunition, then turned to Hilliard, who was leaning against a tree, and said, "You killed Sherd! Now, I'm a-goin' to kill you."

Tilden pointed the gun at the back of Hilliard's head and pulled the trigger. Hilliard bent his head as if in prayer. But the gun didn't go off; it had been fouled when it fell to the ground.

Angry because the gun wouldn't fire, Tilden took the pistol, drew it back level with the ground, and hit Hilliard on the side of the head. Then he hit him on the other side. He kept pistol-whipping him until no one in the group could understand how Hilliard could still sit up—or be alive, for that matter.

Finally, some of his anger satisfied, Tilden stopped. Hilliard had surely been beaten as bad as any man had ever been, but at no time did he fall or even act like he was going to fall. He acted as though he were almost inhuman, or made of unworldly stuff.

With things quieted for the moment, I said to the group, "You men eat if you like, but we've got to get Sherd and Hilliard to town."

We loaded Sherd in the back seat, with the Parson on one side of him and Tilden on the other. Elmer drove the car, and Hilliard sat between Elmer and me in the front seat.

As we started up Granny Maiden Hill, Tilden who now had a pistol that would work, poked the barrel of the gun into the back of Hilliard's bloody head and said, "Hilliard, I got my hand on Sherd's pulse. If it stops beatin', I'm agoin' to pull this trigger and send your soul to hell."

Hilliard was holding his mangled skull and praying, "Oh Lordy, Lordy! Have mercy on me."

I couldn't help but think, as I sat beside him, that if he had just prayed that prayer during the revival, when the Spirit of the Lord was calling him, he wouldn't be in this nightmarish predicament now.

But now the miracle of God's grace began to work!

Elmer, who had beaten Hilliard unmercifully with his blackjack, began to plead with his Uncle Tilden. "Uncle Tilden! Please, listen to me. Don't kill Hilliard! If you do, his blood will be on your hands forever. Don't do it, Uncle Tilden! Please, don't do it!"

When we got to the crest of Granny Maiden's Hill, Sherd gave his last gasp of life. I prayed as I have never prayed, and Elmer continued to beg Tilden not to kill Hilliard.

Sherd slumped lifelessly in the back seat, and Tilden in response to Elmer's pleas, slowly dropped the gun from Hilliard's head. It was all over!

Elmer's prayer had been answered. Although in a fit of rage he had beaten Hilliard badly, he had been able, in his anguish and grief over his father's needless and untimely death, to pray in the spirit of the Master, who in his hour of anguish had prayed: "Father, forgive them for they know not what they do." His prayer too had been answered.

We dropped Hilliard off at the Sheriff's office, and Sherd at the undertaker's.

Elmer, now composed, picked out a casket for his father and made arrangements for the funeral. All through the evening he was calm, serene, and free from the emotion customary in the mountains.

It was late when Elmer finished doing all the necessary things, and we had not eaten. We decided to get a bite before we made the bumpy journey back out to the Settlement. There was a full moon, and the sky was full of stars. We walked down the empty street without talking. We both were so emotionally drained that words did not come easily, and even seemed a bit superfluous.

We finally found a restaurant open. When we had given our order, Elmer broke the silence. "Preacher," he said, "do you know somethun'? I'm mighty proud I didn't kill Hilliard today. Yes, I meant to kill him, but I'm mighty glad I didn't. I wouldn't want his blood on my hands."

What an evening it had been! I never want to live through another like it.

Knowing the code of the hills—the eye-for-an-eye-and-tooth-for-a-tooth philosophy—I could see in Elmer's words evidence that the Parson's work through the years had not been in vain. And I could see that we were right where the Lord wanted us. With men like Elmer on his side, able to forgive the man who, a few hours before, had killed his beloved father, Christ would, I knew, win the battle and solve every problem that came up in those mountains, or anywhere else.

19.

AS THY SOUL PROSPERETH

"Beloved, I wish above all things that thou mayest prosper and be in health, even as thy soul prospereth," the apostle John wrote in his third epistle. But they could well have been written by the Parson. He was ever solicitous of the physical, mental, and spiritual health of the people of Laurel Fork.

Sanitary conditions were not all they should be. Homes were made of crude logs plastered with clay, with many chinks letting daylight through. Windows were virtually unknown. Newspaper was the standard wallpaper, and it did a good job keeping out the cold air in winter. In warm weather, the doors swung open to let a little daylight into the windowless houses. Flies—which seemed to flourish especially well in the mountains—and other insects feasted upon the defenseless mountaineers, who had no money to buy screen doors to keep the winged intruders out. Often the cabins were built on pilings, elevated above the ground four or five feet, to make a place underneath for the pigs, chickens, and other animals. Thus the whole family lived together in close proximity and togetherness. As one mountain boy wrote:

Old Flem

Home was just a two-roomed shack
Of boards laid on logs;
With lots of open space beneath
Where Old Flem raised his hogs.

When Flem told me that his two girls,
And his tow-headed boys,
Slept in that room above the pigs,
I lost my usual poise.

AS THY SOUL PROSPERETH

I said, "Ain't it unhealthy to raise those hogs
Under the bedroom floor?"
Flem slapped a cat out of his plate,
And kicked it through the door.

"Unhealthy, humph," old Flem replied;
"I'll leave it to my wife,
In all these years I've never had
A sick hog in my life."

Some of the families did remarkably well, considering their limited facilities; for example, the Bowlin family. The Bowlins had an even dozen children under their clapboard roof. The seven girls and five boys, along with their outstanding parents, had learned to tolerate existing circumstances and to rise above them. The seven girls attended the Settlement school, and four went on to graduate from high school; these four were especially active in the church and other community projects.

Ethel, a typical member of the Bowlin family, won many honors during her school years; and was granted the highest award by the state 4-H clubs. In spite of her lowly birth, she was selected as the girl to represent the "Spirit of Club Work," the highest possible honor in the 4-H Club.

The health-consciousness of the Settlement was apparent from the very beginning of the work. To treat the soul and neglect the body was for the Parson unthinkable. The Master, who had power both to forgive sins and to heal the sick, had set the example. They had simply followed.

There was never a time when there was not a nurse at the Settlement. Having a nurse was imperative since doctors were so hard to reach. Miss Rhodus, the nurse in 1930, reported her work for that year:

Treated 2,343 person in all. Traveled 1,580 miles on horseback, and 194 miles on foot. 99 children were given diphtheria vaccine, more than 300 were given typhoid serum, five had tonsils removed, two received treatment from the Crippled Children's Commission, four were taken to specialists in

137

Louisville, Kentucky, 19 were taken to county facilities for examinations. One was taken to a distant city for a surgical operation. There were 13 pre-natal, and 10 post-natal cases.

Miss Rhodus arose at 5:30 A.M. and opened her office for medical services, so she would be available to treat people before they went to the mines or other places of work. She had many patients to arrive at this early hour. At 7 A.M., she transferred to her school office, where she treated children for sores, bruises, colds, and other minor ailments.

Sometimes through the years, minor, and even major, miracles occurred in the hills. There was the time when Mrs. H. E. Kingon was the Settlement nurse in 1936. She received a call from Cornett's Branch one morning after a big snowstorm. The trail was almost impassable; but she had heard that the patient was near death so she set out to see what she could do.

So serious was the condition of the sick man that his brother stopped at the Settlement store on his way home from Mrs. Kingon's and bought material to line his coffin. The coffin had already been made by the family and neighbors. No one expected him to live; and the request for Mrs. Kingon to visit him was made because the family wanted the security of having a knowledgeable person standing by as he died.

The man was in a diabetic coma and was all but beyond the reach of medical science. He could not keep food down, and Mrs. Kingon knew he needed his stomach pumped, as it was undoubtedly overloaded with sugar. As she faced the situation, she reasoned that it would take from eight to ten hours to obtain a stomach pump from Middlesboro or Pineville, and that would be too late. She would have to "make do" with something close at hand. She called for a funnel, but none was available. Quickly, she asked some of the relatives to get her a small green gourd, her second choice of a tool.

When they brought it to her, she hollowed it out, attached a small rubber hose to it, and then manipulated the gourd through the man's esophagus and down into his stomach. She then fed him milk through a tube; and in thirty hours, much to everyone's amazement, he was feeling normal.

As a result of this life-saving miracle, the nurse was invited to be the "doctor" at one of the coal mines a few miles away. But better than that, because of her a funeral was cancelled, a casket stored away for future use, and a dying patient pronounced cured.

As one can imagine, there was a crying need for dental work at Laurel Fork. Most of the people had never seen a dentist, nor heard tell of one. The condition of the average mouth was atrocious. Through the cooperation of the County and State health departments, a dental clinic was started at the Settlement on November 15, 1940.

Because of the dangerous condition of the road, Dr. Ballau was unable to bring his dental trailer to Laurel Fork. But, having seen the urgent need for dental care by the people, he detached his equipment, loaded it onto a truck, and brought it to the Settlement. He set up an improvised dental office under the Post Office, and people filed into it hour after hour. They were anxious to get rid of some of their daily toothaches. Fifty-six children had extractions, 175 adults and children had fillings, and 200 mountain people had their teeth cleaned for the first time.

Because there was no doctor at the Settlement, and the existing roads were so impassable, the Settlement nurse did the work of both doctor and nurse. She worked under the guidance of the doctors in Middlesboro, Pruden, and Fonde. When she was uncertain about treatment, the doctors would give her helpful advice.

One annual report shows the scope of the nurse's work.

Treatment to schoolchildren during the term	209
Treatment to dormitory children	211
Outside patients to clinic	1,149
Home visits made	176
Total	1,735

Babies delivered without a physician 14
Babies delivered with a physician 3
Typhoid serum given (3 doses) 373
Blood tests made 22
Classes in Hygiene taught 36
High school girls receiving certificates 11
Mothers' classes held 7
Schoolchildren examined 211

Nearly all the children of Laurel Fork were ushered into the world by the mountain midwife. *Coronet* magazine honored Granny Maiden, the ninety-two-year-old midwife of Laurel Fork, in a featured article. She delivered more than 900 babies in her long career, and was held in high esteem by all the people in the little community. In fact, she was present and active when most of the present population saw the light of day.

One health inspection of 239 children revealed that 80 had tonsil defects, and that 18 needed their tonsils removed immediately. There was talk of having a mass operation, with the doctors of Middlesboro coming out to perform the eighteen tonsillectomies. But, it was decided that it would be far safer and more convenient for the patients to be taken to the Evans Hospital in Middlesboro for the operations. The administrative staff at Evans was most helpful in making the arrangements for the project.

So on a bright Saturday morning, at daylight, eighteen youngsters were loaded into trucks and cars and taken to the hospital. There they all had surgery, and the doctors reported all the operations a success. The next morning the patients were again loaded into the same trucks and cars and returned to the Settlement. They had sore throats, but the project was completed.

When my wife and I joined the staff at the Settlement in 1944, as pastor, coach, music teacher, and medical officer, the first thing we did was to open up a first-aid office in the parsonage. From morning to night we treated patients for blood poisoning, sprained ankles, open wounds, boils, impetigo, headaches, and head colds. The thing that concerned us most was that it took nearly three hours to make the rocky, often dangerous, drive into Pineville or Middlesboro to the nearest medical facilities. When we had an emergency case, it was touch and go: and, in the case of an appendectomy or pregnancy, the roughness of the road made it extremely hazardous.

I owned a single-engine light plane, which I hangared in Middlesboro and used for quick trips to Cincinnati and Indianapolis. No plane had ever landed at Henderson Settlement and, due to the unusually erratic terrain, no one thought that one ever would. But one day as I looked at the little five-acre meadow that sloped down to the creek from the church, I had an idea. I estimated the field to be from 500 to 600 feet in length. However, there was a fence two thirds down the field, making the total distance available for a runway less than 400 feet. I stepped the field off again and again, hoping to discover some way to land a plane in that field. What an asset it would be in an emergency!

I finally decided that on a day when there was little or no wind I could land my plane by coming in toward the church, stalling out just as I got over the fence, and then dropping it in. I figured that after I got the wheels on the ground, I would have 150 to 200 feet to put on the brakes and bring it to a stop. One quiet, windless day, I brought the plane to the Settlement and tried it, and it worked out okay. The only trouble was that in order to get the plane out, I had to take off with the tail of the plane toward the church, and I had that fence (which I found could not be removed) to contend with. I solved that problem by building a "jump" out of logs about 15 feet from the fence. When the plane hit the jump, it sprang into the air momentarily, leaped the fence, and then settled back down almost to the ground; but with careful maneuvering and throttling, the plane could take off. I didn't plan to take it out except on rare occasions or in real emergencies.

John L., who was an alcoholic, provided the first real emergency. Alcoholism was quite prevalent in the valley. Though the people scarcely had enough money to buy the necessities of life for their families, they always seemed to find enough money to buy liquor when they wanted it. Old John L. was a close neighbor of ours, and almost every day would stumble into our medical office for "help." He was really quite starved for love and attention. His wife, who was a good woman, had written John off as a total loss, and considered him completely hopeless.

One day, John L. sent his son for me, as he was very ill. The son was convinced he was dying. It seemed he had gotten some "bad" liquor and was bleeding and suffering from severe stomach cramps. Some mountain purveyors of liquor had no conscience about "watering" their booze down with wood alcohol, or any other concoction that would increase their volume and profits.

I walked the quarter mile down to John L.'s house and found him to be quite drunk and critically ill—not an unusual combination. He knew he was going to die, he said; but he wanted me to get him to a doctor right away. He kept insisting in his miserable condition; so remembering my plane, I classified this the emergency I had been waiting for.

John L., who had scarcely seen an airplane until I landed mine in his back field, was going to take his first plane ride; and bad as things looked, it could well be his last.

I put John L's coat on him, for he was very weak, put my arm around his waist to help him walk, and informed him. "John L., you're right. You need a doctor. I'm going to *fly* you to Middlesboro."

In his weakened state, he didn't really care how he got to the doctor. He just wanted to get there in a hurry. If he had been alert, I never would have gotten him into the plane. But now, instead of fighting his mode of transportation, he said, "Yeah, Preacher, I'm with you. I know you'll do whut's right fer me."

AS THY SOUL PROSPERETH

I loaded John L. into the aircraft, warned him not to touch the controls, and went to crank the engine. With the motor running, I hurried back, climbed into the cockpit, fastened both of our seat belts, and braced myself for the maiden "emergency voyage" out of the Henderson Settlement Municipal Airport.

John L. looked as if he were asleep by this time, so I ignored him, as I held the brakes firmly and opened the throttle wide. Then, as my airspeed came up to maximum, I released the brakes, and we sped down the bumpy meadow toward the jump and the fast-approaching fence. Would the jump work with two grown men and a full load of gasoline? In seconds, we hit the jump, and the plane hurtled into the air. We cleared the fence by a good six inches, and settled back down nearly to the ground again.

By this time, John L. was fully awake and praying loudly, "Oh Lordy! Oh Lordy! Save me! Oh Lordy, save me!"

While John L. in his fear prayed fervently, I said a sincere "amen" to his prayer; for I knew that if the Lord saved him, I would be saved also.

I pushed the throttle into the dashboard and breathed a deep sigh of relief, as the little ship began slowly to gain altitude. The sky was a bit overcast and the visibility was not good, but I saw a patch of blue overhead, and I began to climb toward that little hole in the sky. I bored through it, and as we cleared the cloud cover I could see Middlesboro off to the right. I headed in that direction.

After John L.'s agonizing prayer, he kept his head down so he wouldn't have to see what was really happening. It appeared he either lacked faith in his prayer or his pilot. As he felt the plane level off, he dared to glance out the window momentarily. He saw Middlesboro, bathed in sunlight, in the distance; and in his stupor he must have thought it was the pearly white city for he began to moan, "Oh Lordy, we're in heaven; Oh Lordy, I'm out of this world! Oh Lordy, Lordy!"

"No, John," I reluctantly told him, "that's Middlesboro."

John shook his head unbelievingly and stammered, "Preacher, if that's Middlesboro, what am I doin' up here?"

After an uneventful landing, I finally got John L. out of the plane and on to the hospital. They kept him overnight and pumped his stomach out, and I took him back the next day in the little plane.

The experience, so wild and unusual, so traumatic and unbelievable, so out-of-this-world, made quite an impression on John L. As I helped him out of the plane, he said: "Preacher, I'm a-tellin' you the truth! I'll never drink another drop of liquor as long as I live. You've helped me ta' see the light." He then put his arm around me and sobbed out his gratitude.

The little ambulance-plane became quite an asset in frequent emergencies; and the trial run had given me the confidence I needed to use it. Perhaps it was good that our first emergency was for a drunk, for we used it often after that without a single mishap.

20.

THE GLORY ROAD

Roads are the outreach of the people. Isolation is a good thing for awhile, but no person or group can be shut off from the world forever. When there are no roads, the bad cannot get out, and the good cannot get in.

The Laurel Fork community had no roads, in the real sense of the word. An Indian trail had been blazed more than a hundred years ago from Pineville, through Chenoa, and on through Laurel Fork. When people went to town, as even the most isolated people must do occasionally, they rode mules, or in mule-pulled wagons, over the rough, rocky clearings mistakenly called the "Pineville Road." The dangerous situation that existed when someone at Laurel Fork was very ill and needed to be taken to the doctor has already been mentioned. The lack of a proper road also kept law officers from ever "lookin' in " on the little community. Hence, the poor road made for lawlessness, for inconvenience, and, in the case of serious illness or a shooting, stark tragedy.

From the very outset Frakes campaigned for a road to the Settlement, but he had two or perhaps three strikes against him. First, there were so few people in this remote valley that they provided very little political patronage. There were only about 1,500 persons in the Laurel Fork community, if you counted women (who seldom voted) and children. Second, most of the people who did vote were staunch Republicans, while most of the county and state politicians were controlled by the stronger Democratic Party. And third, there were few residences on the old Pineville Road, as the people were hidden back in the little coves, ravines, etc. So the cost of building a road for so few was so expensive that it was simply out of the question.

When Frakes talked about his plan to get a road, the local men just looked at each other with a wry smile, as if to say, "Now the Parson is dreaming another *big* one. There'll never be a road in these parts."

But the Parson was as tenacious as a bulldog, when he got an idea into his head that something ought to be done. He had traveled those muddy, dangerous, rut-filled roads on mule, in a wagon, and in an old Jeep, but he didn't plan to do that all his life. For the Settlement was growing, and he had faith to believe that someday there would be a beautiful graded and paved road from Pineville to Laurel Fork.

Every time he met a state official, he told him of his people and their progress, and got in his strong pitch for a new road. They all admitted the need but shied away from the responsibility of the deed.

By 1945, twenty years after the founding of the Settlement, Frakes was tired of being put off on the road project. That year Kentucky had a Republican governor, which was rare. To put his desperate plan in action, Frakes contacted all the Republican county officials, and asked them to accompany him to Frankfort to see the State Highway Commissioner about getting a road built. After he and his cordon of officials had presented their case to the governor, the governor said, "I'm sorry, gentlemen, we do not have the money in the state funds for such a project; but if the Federal Government would help, we could do it."

That was about the time that the Federal Government was starting to help the states with their roads and highways.

After Frakes returned to Bell County and Laurel Fork, the germ of an idea came to him. Although he had been a strong Republican, he was not above switching horses in the middle of the stream if his cause could be better served. He knew an influential Democrat in Pineville, and he made the trip into the county seat to see him. After a brief but effective visit, Frakes persuaded the man to accompany him to Washington to see the Democratic Senator from their district. Frakes knew the Senator well, and was convinced that he would be sympathetic to the project.

The country preacher and the small-town politician knocked on the door of the esteemed Senator's plush office; rarely had he been approached by a better combination of grit, grace, and guts. To their delight the Senator was in an approachable mood—perhaps because an election was in the offing, and he needed to garner every possible vote to defeat the rather formidable young man who was his opponent and be reelected. The Senator waved the two men into his well-appointed office.

"Glad to see you, Frakes," the Senator greeted him. Then he spoke to the politician with Frakes for a few minutes about the political condition of their state. When they had concluded their few remarks, he asked, "What can I do for you men?"

"Our mission is simple," Frakes began, "so I'll be brief, for I know you are a very busy man. I've been working with the poor people of your district down in Bell County for twenty years now. I guess you aren't aware of it, but I'm sure we have the poorest roads in the entire commonwealth of Kentucky. What we need and want, Senator, is to have that old muddy, rutted trail from Pineville through Chenoa to Laurel Fork, graded and paved."

The Senator was a little astonished at the bigness of Frakes's wish. He looked at him with a sly grin and said, "Preacher, I'm led to believe you believe in that Scripture that says, 'Ask largely that your joy may be full.'"

Frakes was very serious in his reply. "You bet I do, Senator! I believe every word in the Bible, and I'm trusting that you believe it too."

"Do you know what you're asking for, man?" the Senator asked. "You're talking about a half-million dollars or more, and that's a lot of money for those few voters down there, especially since most of them are Republicans."

"Your honor," Frakes persisted, "Republicans hate mud, ruts, and jagged rocks just as much as Democrats. Their kids get sick and have to be taken to the hospital, and their women need obstetricians just the same as city women. And as long as we're isolated from the County Seat by impassable roads, there will continue to be killings and lawlessness in that area. Senator, we need a road, and we need it bad!"

The Senator sat and studied his knuckles for a moment; and then, without saying a word in answer to Frakes's argument, he reached for his phone and asked his secretary to get the head of the Department of Federal Highways on the line. When she got the man on the phone, the Senator got right down to business.

He said, "I have two friends here from my state and district. They want to see you about a road project in Bell County. There seems to be a real need. I'm sending them over to your office right now, and anything you can do for them will be considered a personal favor to me."

Frakes knew this was definite progress, and he thanked the Senator profusely before he and the politician hurried away to meet the Commissioner of the Department of Federal Highways.

The Commissioner was waiting for them in his office, which in itself was no small miracle, and they went right in. Usually such contacts take weeks or months. Again Frakes desperately presented his plea for a road, describing the urgent needs. He put special emphasis on the lawlessness of the mountain people, which was a known fact, and charged that isolation was the prime reason. When he had finished his graphic appeal, he waited with bated breath for the Commissioner's judgment.

There was no hesitation on the Commissioner's part. He said, "Gentlemen, it sounds to me like you need and deserve a road. Let me see what I can do. I must contact the Department of Highways' office in Chicago, and the one in Lexington, Kentucky. It shouldn't take me more than two or three days to have the whole project cleared. If you could wait here in Washington for that period, I feel we can send you back with some assurances that your work will someday he rewarded with a road."

With a great sigh of relief and a wide smile, Frakes assured the Commissioner that he'd be glad to wait, however long it took. The two men shook the Commissioner's hand and tried to express their appreciation, and left the office rejoicing. This was indeed one of Frakes's biggest answers to prayer.

In three days, they returned home. The Commissioner had kept his word and gotten right to work; and he was able to give them the good news that the project had been okayed by all concerned.

"Tell your governor that he will receive a proposal from us regarding your road within the next few days," the Commissioner told the men as they were leaving.

Frakes and his Democratic friend made the trip back to Bell County with happy hearts. The dream of twenty years was about to come true.

But there was still some maneuvering to do.

As soon as Frakes got back to Bell County, before sharing his secret with anyone, he switched political horses once more, rallied his Republican friends, and went to Frankfort to see the Republican Governor again. Frakes shared the good news with him. The Governor was astonished that this little man could have accomplished so much. He stood to his feet, came from behind the big desk, and, chuckling, put out his hand to Frakes: "Preacher, I want to shake your hand! That's really great! I didn't think you, or anyone else, could do it."

On Friday, August 23, 1946, Hiram Frakes was invited to Frankfort, Kentucky, to the State Highway Commissioner's office, to sit in on the road lettings, and to hear the bids for road contracts. When the bids were made and the contracts signed insuring the road from Pineville to Henderson Settlement, Frakes breathed a prayer thanking

God. He had waited twenty-one years for this moment. He had traveled that almost-impossible road in the most adverse weather conditions, and to the danger of his own life, too many times to be counted. Those perilous trips would soon be over. They had been worth making, for they had brought life, health, and happiness to the people he loved. But now a new day was dawning, and it would surely be easier now to do his God-given duties.

His faith had taken on "concrete" form (pardon the pun), and grace was to be changed to gravel, testings to tar, and an aesthetic dream into a hard road.

Little wonder that when the long-anticipated road was finally completed, they called it the "Frakes Trail." It was one more tribute to a man whose philosophy was: Dream great things; expect great things from God!

21.

SUNDOWN ON LAUREL FORK

A news item on the front page of the *Middles-boro Daily News,* February 7, 1963, read:

> The Rev. Hiram M. Frakes, 74 years old, founder of Henderson Settlement, now known as Frakes, Kentucky, leaves Bell County this week to end an era.

With nothing but courage and determination, Frakes took education, evangelism, and civilization to an area that had known much moonshining and senseless bloodshed. He built the Settlement from a one-room schoolhouse to its present 22 buildings and over 750 acres of land.

Frakes, for forty-one years, during the years from 1922 to 1963, had witnessed miracle after miracle. He had seen the people of Laurel Fork community shift from moonshining and hog-raising to church-going, school-attending, and respectability. He saw the first drop-reaper unloaded in the valley; the first scientifically planted apple orchard; the first field of wheat; the first clover field; the first cattle testing; the first modern houses; the first up-to-date school; the first boarding school; the first honor students; the first college graduates; the first Men's Brotherhood; the first 4-H Club; the first rural mail service; the first paved road to Laurel Fork community; the first airplane; the first machine shop; the first tractor; the first basketball team; the first planned revival; the first community celebrations; the first Laurel Fork Fair; and the first full year without a murder in the community. Firsts, firsts, firsts! Frakes had seen all these and many more.

Perhaps the reason for these great accomplishments was that the Parson took the words of the Christ he served literally: "Seek ye first the kingdom of God, and all these things will be added unto you." They had been added, in abundance.

Frakes never once dreamed, when he visited Washington with his quartette one year, that they would be received and commended by President Herbert Hoover. Elmer Partin, Wayland Jones, Mabel Henderson, and Ethel and Margie Bowlin stood in the White House garden with the President, and the chief executive seemed in no hurry to leave their company. He was full of praises for the work of Henderson Settlement.

Governors, judges, and bishops had graced the Settlement grounds, and had participated in various celebrations and ceremonies. National magazines had taken note of the significant accomplishments of the Parson and his staff. *Life,* one of the leading news magazines of the nation, had sent their entire photographic and editorial staff to cover an event in the community.

But, for Frakes, the greatest achievement was the progress of the people. One Sunday morning, he looked out over the audience in Kynett Chapel (named for Dr. A. G. Kynett, onetime secretary of the church extension department) and counted twelve men who had once been moonshiners, who were now faithful members of the church. As he saw them there, dressed in their Sunday best, sitting with their families, singing, praying, and worshiping together, he knew it had all been worthwhile.

He thought of the many souls that had been saved, and of the many lives that had been changed. In this area, where bloodshed had been a weekly affair, violence was now more rare than in well-policed Middlesboro and Pineville.

Even the men of those mountains who had not embraced religion were kindly disposed to the Parson. They knew him to be a man not only concerned for their souls, but also for their total welfare. One of them remarked after attending one of the church services, "I ain't got much religion; but when I git it, I'm goin' to put it here."

Frakes had seen the men who gave him the land to get started pass on to their reward—Bill Henderson, Uncle Scott Partin, Sherd Partin, and the others. He had conducted most of their funerals. Before they died, they all had seen the fruits of their sacrifice. There was not a man who regretted what he had given.

Frakes had seen political elections—which used to be bloody affairs—conducted honestly and peacefully without the slightest incident.

He had seen infant mortality, once so high in the hills, go down tremendously. And he had brought medical services to the valley to fight disease, malnutrition, and human suffering of all kinds.

On the twenty-fifth anniversary of the Settlement, people gathered from far and near to pay honor to Frakes and the One he served. The famous and the unknown were there, as well as the rich and the poor. As the old-timers, like one-hundred-three-year-old Uncle Harvey Sparks and the aged artisan Scott Partin and his wife, reminisced about the past, Frakes took out his big white handerchief and dabbed the moisture from his eyes. He remembered well the tales they told.

Ex-governor Flem D. Sample talked about the miracle of turning liquor into groceries, and lethargy and violence into peace. "It is indisputably one of the miracles of our age," he told the people.

A chorus of two hundred schoolchildren and one hundred mountain folk sang, "God Bless America." When they came to the words, "From the mountains to the prairies, / To the ocean white with foam," hearts beat a little faster. For in that audience was a crowd of people who had come to know what it really means to be Americans—with all the attendant advantages.

Finally Frakes himself took the podium. His voice was familiar to the people. They had heard it in frankness and in compassion. They had heard that voice say once, when gun-toting was still in vogue in the valley and several men sat in the audience wearing holsters with guns in them: "You folks think it is a sign of bravery to carry pistols. You are mistaken! It is a sign of cowardice. You are afraid of someone, or you wouldn't carry a pistol. I carry no pistol, and I'm not afraid of anyone. I carry my own weapon, a two-edged sword, the Bible, and that's all the protection I need."

One man, who had been carrying a pistol, had two bullet holes in his hat where someone had shot at him from ambush. He went home and considered Frakes's sermon, and later said to his wife, "The Parson said this mornin' thet anyone who carried a pistol is a coward. I ain't no coward!" With those words he took off his holster and gun and put them on the mantle, for keeps.

So, when Frakes spoke, the people listened. They trusted him, and, besides, he usually had something worthwhile to say.

He began, "I am reminded today of a passage of Scripture, which was used by our Lord Jesus Christ when he came to his own people in Nazareth. He said: 'The Spirit of the Lord is upon me, because he hath anointed me to preach the Gospel to the poor; he hath sent me to heal the brokenhearted, to preach deliverance to the captives and the recovering of sight to the blind, to set at liberty them that are bruised, to preach the acceptable year of the Lord.'

"As Christ's minister, I have come to you today in his spirit to declare unto you the 'acceptable year of the Lord' and to tell you of better things that can come to you in his name. I can see you living in fine houses with all the blessings and comforts that others have. We have seen great progress, but the work has just begun. I can see this valley becoming the most beautiful part of this county, filled with friendly neighbors and Christian homes, and having God's love filling it as the waters fill the sea."

Always his was the vision celestial—and it was a continuing one—filled with what someone has called "divine discontent" with things as they are. As long as one child was undernourished; one man held hatred in his heart; one person was addicted to alcohol; one child was deprived of an education; or one person needed medical aid, the Parson was discontented.

Frakes had his Brady Miracle, Mabel Henderson, Wayland Jones, Ethel Bowlin, Elmer Partin, and many more. Of the hundreds of kids that had graduated from the school, scores had gone on to college and successful careers. Their lot had been bettered, and, beyond that, they had found Him who said, "I am come that they might have life, and that they might have it more abundantly." That was it: they had, through the prayers and plans of the concerned Parson, found abundant life.

No wonder Mabel Henderson, the daughter of the man for whom the Settlement was named, wrote the school song this way:

> Henderson, our beloved Alma Mater,
>   We'll follow thy teachings each day;
> We'll hold dear thy sweet memories
>   No matter where fate leads the way.
>
> Praises ring from vales and from hills,
>   To crown thee with worship and song;
> We stand at thy shrine with humble hearts,
>   To you our praise and honor belong.
>
> Chorus:
>
> Thy image be engraved on us apart,
>   Thy spirit doth dwell in every heart;
> And though we wander far,
>   You'll be where e'er we are,
> To guide our footsteps should we stray apart.
>   The path way of knowledge
> You have led us through.
>   The blest Golden Rule
> You've taught us well to do.
>   You've held for us the light;
> We'll strive to do the right
>   O Alma Mater, beautiful and true.

In 1969, the Parson, then eighty-one years of age, was called back to Frakes for a latecoming honor. The road department had fashioned a bronze plaque, which was installed on U. S. Highway 25 adjacent to the Bert Combs Forestry Building. It was the latest in the long list of honors which had been accorded him. The plaque stands there for posterity to read, pointing to that larger evidence of his life's work: Henderson Settlement, 17 miles away.

HENDERSON SETTLEMENT

Rev. Hiram M. Frakes founded this Methodist settlement in 1925. Begun in a log cabin with 13 students, it became an institution for spiritual and educational development of mountain youth. Frakes guided and influenced the entire Middle Laurel Fork Valley. Their simply expressed gratitude for his work was: "Parson, we're glad you came."

Monuments were many in the Parson's life. Stone buildings, concrete roads, postal improvements, chapels and churches fashioned of wood, improvements in agriculture and economics—all were monuments. But vastly more important that these are the "living monuments," the people in Laurel Fork community who, through the Parson's efforts, have found a quality of life that will live on after these material objects have wasted away.

People, not wealth or popularity, were his real commodity and product. People like Clyde Davis, a mountain waif whose parents had died and left him homeless. He was taken in by the Parson, who raised him in his own home as he would have his own child, had he had children of his own. Clyde achieved a distinguished record in the armed services of his country, and was given many awards.

People like Wayland Jones, a renegade of a kid who came to the Settlement for help. Homeless, too, Wayland was representative of the hundreds, yes thousands, of mountain children whom the Parson befriended. In an address over WLW, the Nation's Station, Wayland said to an audience of millions:

> I tremble when I think what in all probability would have been my fate if it had not been for the Henderson Settlement School. The Parson picked me up when I was fourteen and set me on a new road of life. I was going the way of most mountain boys, drinking, gambling, and engaging in illicit liquor business. Today, by the grace of God, I am a humble follower of the lowly Nazarene, with a deep desire in my heart to train for effective and efficient leadership . . . my own mountain people.

Wayland's prayer and dream came true, for today he is the coach at Henderson Settlement, and the High School counselor to hundreds of children at the flourishing Henderson Settlement School.

For forty years the Parson had associated with children and young people. He thought young, looked young, and acted young, even in his seventies. Little wonder then, when his first wife passed away, in due time he went "courting"—and of all people, Rebecca Arend Duke, a girl who used to be in the Sunday school he superintended up in Quincy, Indiana. It is difficult to imagine a seventy-year-old "running out of gas" on a car ride through an isolated state park in Indiana, but Rebecca said the Parson did. At eighty-three, the Parson and Rebecca live together happily, in Indiana in the summer and in Florida in the winter, with vacations at Henderson Settlement several times each year.

157

FIRE IN THE HILLS

This story is, of course, unfinished. It is a miracle that will unfold for years and decades to come. We say with the old mountaineer, once the Parson's most bitter enemy, who was wooed and won by his compassion and concern: "Parson, we're mighty glad you came to Laurel Fork."